ALA Editions • **SPECIAL REPORTS**

PRIVATIZING
LIBRARIES

JANE JERRARD, NANCY BOLT, AND KAREN STREGE

FOREWORD BY
PATRICIA A. TUMULTY
Chair, ALA Committee on Library Advocacy
and ALA Task Force on Privatization

AND

MARCI MEROLA
Director, ALA Office for Library Advocacy

AMERICAN LIBRARY ASSOCIATION
Chicago 2012

Jane Jerrard is an independent author and editor based in Chicago. She has written books for consumers, children, and librarians, including the 2009 ALA Special Report *Crisis in Employment: A Librarian's Guide to Helping Job Seekers.*

Nancy Bolt was State Librarian in Colorado for eighteen years, leaving in 2005 to form her own library consulting company, Nancy Bolt & Associates. Since 2006 she has been Project Co-Director for the ALA's Library Support Staff Certification Program. This book is her second project involving privatization of public libraries. She assisted in the development of *Keeping Public Libraries Public: A Checklist for Communities Considering Privatization of Public Libraries.* Bolt has a Master of Library Science from the University of Missouri and just received her certification as an advanced strategic planner from the Association of Strategic Planning.

Karen Strege is a co-director of ALA's Library Support Staff Certification Program and a private library consultant, specializing in evaluation. This is her second project on the privatization of public libraries; she assisted in the development of the Checklist on Privatization for Public Libraries. Strege was the State Librarian in Montana for nine years. She has a Master of Library Science from the University of Washington and a PhD from Gonzaga University in Spokane.

Printed in the United States of America

16   15   14   13   12   5   4   3   2   1

Extensive effort has gone into ensuring the reliability of the information in this book; however, the publisher makes no warranty, express or implied, with respect to the material contained herein.

ISBNs: 978-0-8389-1154-9 (paper); 978-0-8389-9408-5 (PDF); 978-0-8389-9409-2 (ePUB); 978-0-8389-9410-8 (Mobipocket); 978-0-8389-9411-5 (Kindle). For more information on digital formats, visit the ALA Store at alastore.ala.org and select eEditions.

Library of Congress Cataloging-in-Publication Data

Available at http://catalog.loc.gov

Series cover design by Casey Bayer.
Series text design in Palatino Linotype and Avenir by Karen Sheets de Gracia.

♾ This paper meets the requirements of ANSI/NISO Z39.48-1992
(Permanence of Paper).

CONTENTS

ACKNOWLEDGMENTS

The authors would like to thank all the librarians, state library staff, board members, governing officials, data coordinators, and others who generously shared their knowledge and time for the case studies in this publication.

For over two hundred years, public libraries have earned the respect of the residents they serve. Public libraries have been viewed as a public good—a common resource available to all. However, in the past ten years city and county government bodies are increasingly considering the privatization of public libraries—that is, transferring library management and operations from a government agency to a commercial company.

Public libraries have a unique role in the community—that of providing a broad range of services to sustain a well-informed and well-educated public. Libraries are, indeed, the great equalizer—connecting people to information, providing access to twenty-first-century technologies, preserving our history, and cultivating our future, all without regard for background or means. The library is an institution that embodies the American dream like no other.

As local officials are forced to make tough choices, they should understand the full scope of services their libraries offer and the impact libraries have on their communities. If considering privatization of a public library, they must be ready to answer the following difficult questions:

- Can a private company maintain the level of public trust that has been earned by the local library?
- Will the library director always make the operational decisions that are in the best interest of the community, even if those decisions reduce or do not contribute to the private company's profit?
- Does the relationship between a public library and its community change when a library is privatized?
- Does the role of the library as a public good change when the library is privatized?

The American Library Association affirms that policy making and management oversight of public libraries should remain securely in the public domain. It formally adopted a policy against privatization in 2001. As economic conditions have changed and privatization of public services has increased, a new Task Force on Privatization was formed in spring of 2011 to assist library supporters in addressing the issue. The task force cited the quality of library services, loss of local community and government control, loss of control of tax dollars, intellectual freedom, collection development, and loss of community involvement with foundations, Friends groups, and other nonprofit partners as the most crucial issues at stake. Among the most pressing messages that need to be conveyed to decision makers and stakeholders are these:

- There are certain community services that should be held by the public. Libraries are one of them.
- The public should be kept in public libraries. Privatizing the library threatens two pillars of public control: accountability and transparency.
- Decisions made regarding public library services should be driven by the best interests of the community and not driven by profit.
- The notion that privatization saves money is often a false one: hidden and uncontrolled costs may not save money in the long run.
- Apparent reductions in labor costs may be offset by increases in legal costs resulting from employment actions.
- Professional standards and quality of service may be at risk with privatized service.

Privatizing Libraries: A Special Report builds on ALA's *Keeping Public Libraries Public: A Checklist for Communities Considering Privatization of Public Libraries.* This report examines trends and statistics in privatization, presents case studies of privatized public libraries across the country, and—we hope—will assist the library community in informing decision makers about the need to keep this critical public institution in the hands of the public.

Patricia A. Tumulty, Chair, ALA Committee
on Library Advocacy and ALA Task
Force on Privatization

Marci Merola, Director,
ALA Office for Library Advocacy

INTRODUCTION

When did privatization of public services begin? Some say it was when Alexander the Great "privatized" his army, but in the United States we know that as early as 1826 New York City privatized its street sweeping.[1] But the privatization trend this country is currently experiencing began much more recently, in the 1980s, with the strong support of president Ronald Reagan—influenced by U.K. prime minister Margaret Thatcher. While Thatcher was implementing national privatization initiatives in her country, Reagan was primarily a cheerleader for privatization efforts in Eastern bloc countries. His administration did, however, establish the President's Commission on Privatization in 1987, and it privatized the railroad that the federal government acquired from bankrupt Penn-Central, creating ConRail.[2]

By the end of the 1980s, the idea that privatizing services and assets could reduce government's size and potentially save costs and increase efficiency had gained traction. And when the 2008 recession squeezed state and local governments, more and more of them privatized their assets and services either to cut payroll and other service costs or to realize a sudden increase of ready cash through leaseback deals. A combination of tight budgets and low reserves in cities, counties, and states and a wave of conservatism that values smaller government contributed to a flourishing of privatization.

In 1993, in response to increased privatization efforts (some of which were suspected of involving cronyism and lack of competition), the Massachusetts legislature passed the Pacheco Law, which requires the state auditor to conduct a cost-benefit analysis on any proposal to privatize the state's services or assets.[3] The state auditor reviews each application for privatization to determine if the cost of the outsourced service would be less than that performed by the government while maintaining the same quality of service or better. The same year, the Washington, D.C., city council passed a similar law, which states that the government must prove it would save at least 10 percent over the contract's duration, and that, if hired, the contractor must offer all displaced employees comparable employment for six months.[4]

A SNAPSHOT OF PRIVATIZATION TODAY

Every ten years, the International City-County Management Association (ICMA) tracks privatization of resources. Its most recent survey, released in 2007, reviewed sixty-seven local services in more than a thousand U.S. municipalities.[5] The report shows that, of these public services, 17 percent were handled through for-profit privatization, with 16 percent provided through intergovernmental contracting (i.e., the county may handle some municipal services). According to this study the most common local services that are contracted out include waste collection, waste disposal, management of vehicle fleets, hospitals, vehicle towing, electric utilities, drug programs, and emergency medical service—among many others.

Slightly more than 50 percent of respondents to the 2007 ICMA survey said that their local government had "studied the feasibility of adopting private service delivery within the past five years." Those respondents indentified the following reasons for considering privatization:

86.7%	Internal attempts to decrease costs of service delivery
50.3%	External fiscal pressures, including restrictions placed on raising taxes, e.g., California Proposition 13 of 1978
15.9%	Unsolicited proposals presented by potential service providers
14.0%	Change in political climate emphasizing a decreased role for government
10.1%	Concerns about government liability
9.9%	State or federal mandates tied to intergovernment financing
3.9%	Active citizen group favoring privatization
12.1%	Other

(The total percentage is over 100 percent because respondents could select all applicable reasons.)

These responses provide a concise summary of why local governments today look to privatize assets—to decrease costs and ease budget restrictions. Asked if their government had returned any previously privatized services to public management in the previous five years, 78.4 percent answered yes. Of those, respondents identified the following factors in the decision:

61.2%	Service quality not satisfactory
52.4%	Cost savings insufficient
33.9%	Local government efficiency improved
17.0%	Problems monitoring the contract
17.0%	Strong political support to bring back the service delivery
10.0%	Problems with the contract specifications
13.3%	Other

Today, the number of local governments considering private management of public assets is steadily increasing, and it is becoming more common for those assets to include the public library. This special report takes a close look at what this entails, including the effects on specific libraries and communities, and provides advice to readers on how to handle efforts to privatize their libraries.

NOTES

1. Moshe Adler, "In City Services, Privatize and Beware," *New York Times on the Web*, April 7, 1996, www.columbia.edu/~ma820/privatization.nyt.html.

2. Robert W. Poole Jr., "Ronald Reagan and the Privatization Revolution," *Heartlander*, August 1, 2004, www.heartland.org/policybot/results/15469/Ronald_Reagan_and_the _Privatization_Revolution.html.

3. "Privatization: The Real Story," Working Massachusetts, http://workingmass.org/ privatization-real-story.

4. "Anti-Privatization Initiatives," New Rules Project, www.newrules.org/governance/rules/ antiprivatization-initiatives.

5. ICMA, *Profile in Local Government Service Delivery Choices* (Washington, DC: ICMA, 2007).

1
PRIVATIZATION OF PUBLIC LIBRARIES: AN OVERVIEW

For various reasons, local and state governments across the United States are privatizing selected assets and services, with decidedly mixed, often unclear, results. From the late 1990s to the present day, this trend has expanded into the public library sector, as local governments look to private companies to fulfill essential management responsibilities traditionally met by public employees.

PRIVATIZATION DEFINED

Historically, *privatization* referred specifically to the transfer of ownership from the public sector, or government, to the private sector—a for-profit or in some cases nonprofit organization. In recent times the definition has been broadened to include the transfer of *function,* or management, of public assets, services, facilities, and agencies, including everything from contracting out management of a city's water sanitization to hiring a private company to provide a community's emergency medical services.[1] This latter definition is the type of privatization covered in this book, and it occurs at the local, state, and federal level.

The Public Library Association (PLA), a division of ALA, used the following definitions in its 2000 report on privatization. The definition of privatization derived from the 1998 deliberations of ALA's Outsourcing Task Force.

> **Outsourcing** involves transfer to a third-party or outside vendor, or contractor, or independent workers, or provider to perform certain work-related tasks involving recurring internal activities that are not core to the mission of the library.

> **Privatization** is the shifting of library service from the public to the private sector through transference of library management and/or assets from a government agency to a commercial company.

Some in the library community suggest that there is no difference between the two. They argue that in outsourcing a third party provides a service and makes a profit just as in privatization. But one of the main differences is that in outsourcing the contract is typically narrow, encompassing an easily defined, specific service that is easily monitored—such as cataloging or standing orders with a book jobber. In these cases, the private company decides *how* a service is delivered but the publicly funded library staff controls, via contract, what those services are. Privatization takes outsourcing to another level—involving all library services and including not only *how* services are delivered but *which* services are offered and delivered.

Pro-privatization individuals in the library community routinely argue that privately managed public libraries are not privatized because the authority to approve library policy and the title to assets remain "public." In fact, in every privately managed library we researched, the library's governing body did retain authority over policy approval. But policy creation and policy approval are two different tasks, and the power to frame a policy, along with its rationale and operational implications, typically rests with library management, whether that management is public or private.

The library's *assets* are typically defined in business literature as having tangible and intangible elements. The tangible elements include facilities, inventory, and equipment. Intangible assets include the organization's brand, goodwill, public opinion, and service delivery. In library privatization contracts, the governing body retains ownership of tangible assets, but the private company controls their operation and, for equipment and resources, the selection as well. The intangible assets are completely in the control of the private company.

ALA AND STATE POLICIES ON PRIVATIZATION

After considering the issues of outsourcing and privatization in 2001, the ALA Council voted to adopt the following policy:

> ALA affirms that publicly funded libraries should remain directly accountable to the public they serve. Therefore, the ALA opposes the shifting of policymaking and management oversight of library services from the public to the private for-profit sector.

The PLA report characterizes the opposing positions regarding outsourcing of public library management:

> Proponents maintain that outsourcing [of library management] offers unique opportunities to reduce costs and capitalize on the investments, innovations, and special capabilities of external suppliers. . . . Opponents maintain that outsourcing of core functions threatens public library institutional viability, diverts local control, and diminishes the contributed value of professional librarians.

In addition to the ALA policies, state libraries and state library associations have issued statements on privatization or outsourcing. For example, the Florida Library Association took a strong position against privatization in 1999, stating that "it is not in the best interest of the residents of Florida for publicly supported libraries to be managed by for-profit organizations. Therefore the Association opposes any efforts to provide library services by contracting with such organization."[2]

New Jersey adopted its Statement on Outsourcing Public Library Services in 1998 and revised it in 2001. It states in part that any decisions on outsourcing management of public library service should be governed by six criteria and concludes, "It is the position of the New Jersey Library Association that outsourcing the management of a public library is a most serious step and should only be undertaken after careful study and as a last resort."[3]

The Massachusetts Board of Library Commissions published *Privatization of Public Libraries: A List of Information Resources* to help public libraries sort through the issues related to privatization. The document includes a short list of Massachusetts laws pertaining to public libraries that must be followed for a privatized library to continue to receive state benefits.[4]

California has had much privatization activity, with five library systems covering forty-three branch libraries under private management. In 2011, with active union support, California passed a bill dictating that cities or library districts that intend to contract with a private company to manage a public library must meet specific benchmarks: offer public notice, demonstrate cost savings for the duration of the contract, participate in competitive bidding, and prove the qualifications of the contractor. The California Library Association (CLA) took a "watch" position on this bill, basically neither endorsing nor opposing it. In doing so they made the following statement:

> CLA absolutely believes that, under most circumstances, public libraries are a critical community resource that should be just that: public. Nevertheless, we also note that limiting local government's ability to manage resources during the current challenging economic climate is almost certain to result in the reduction or elimination of library services. While many CLA members work for city governments that are actively opposing the bill, many CLA members are also members of SEIU or other local unions. We also recognize that employees of LSSI—the only private provider of library services in the U.S.—are CLA members.[5]

California's position reflects the tension within the library community of being responsive to local government's concerns about library service and the desire to keep the library publicly managed. It raises the question, Is privatized library service better than no library service at all?

STATE OF LIBRARY PRIVATIZATION

As of August 2011, seventeen public library systems in five states had contracts with a private management company. An additional six had such contracts but have returned to public management. The number of communities in the United States—and in Canada and the United Kingdom—considering privatizing the public library seems to be increasing every month.

To date, only one company, Library Systems & Services, LLC (LSSI), contracts with public libraries for management services. Based in Maryland, LSSI is majority owned by a private equity firm called Islington Capital Partners, has approximately 800 employees, and earns about $35 million in annual revenue.[6] Historically, the company has provided management and outsourcing services for libraries in schools, colleges, corporations, and the federal government. Now that the privatization trend has gained momentum, the company's website indicates that its focus has narrowed to acquiring new customers in that sector.

At least two other companies have submitted proposals to manage public libraries, but neither has managed yet to break into the market. Ron Dubberly, president of LSSI, says his company would welcome competitors: "Competition is healthy, it's good for our customers, and I would welcome it."

A BRIEF HISTORY

The trend of privatizing public libraries started in 1997, when California's Riverside County Library System contracted with LSSI. This system remains LSSI's largest and oldest public library customer. With the Riverside County contract, the concept of a private company providing complete management services for a library became a reality. As the library community gradually became aware of the practice and the vendor, more communities began following Riverside's lead.

In 2010 and 2011, media attention and industry discussions of privatizing public libraries grew tremendously because of a contentious decision by the City of Santa Clarita, California, to bid out the management of its newly independent library. The arguments for and against privatizing Santa Clarita's library—and privatizing public libraries in general—raged on library industry blogs, in the general media, and, doubtless, throughout many library board meetings around the country. Santa Clarita's city council voted to privatize in spite of strong and very vocal public resistance, and LSSI began managing its libraries in July 2011. With the addition of Santa Clarita, seventeen public library systems, comprising seventy-one libraries, were being managed by a private company.

WHY LOCAL GOVERNMENTS CONSIDER PRIVATIZATION

Each city, county, or library board (governing body) has different reasons for exploring privatization. All, however, can be summarized by four themes:

New independence. The governing body withdrew its community library from a larger district or system and established a new independent library. The governing body sought professional expertise to guide it in starting a library, and a private company filled that need.

Inability to staff. The governing body was unsuccessful at recruiting or retaining a library director who would commit to the community. Contracting with a private company ensured the library would remain staffed.

Poor opinion of library. Some or all members of the governing body held a poor opinion of the library administration and did not or could not change that administration. Some governing bodies had serious policy differences with the library director about the library's direction. These bodies viewed privatization as a way to eliminate unacceptable library administration, because problematic employees were not offered employment by the private contractor.

Budget constraints. In communities with reduced or severely limited budgets, local government sought ways to continue service for less money.

HOW LIBRARY PRIVATIZATION OCCURS

The wide range of public libraries currently under private management demonstrates that there are no set parameters for privatization. LSSI's Dubberly confirms this, saying, "It's not about size; it's about fit and what [LSSI] can offer."

In most cases we found that the idea for privatizing originated with the governing body rather than the library board or staff. Members of city and county government belong to professional associations and attend regional and national conferences, just as librarians do, and there they share ideas. Networking with other government officials may be their main avenue for learning about privatizing public libraries, and specifically about LSSI. "Typically we go to city/county conferences and let them know we're there," says Dubberly. "They come by [the LSSI booth] to talk to us. Occasionally we get calls." He confirms that the number of interested communities has grown recently but says that each has a different reason for considering private library management.

Some librarians have stated that LSSI "cold-calls" local governments to pitch their services, but Dubberly stresses that "the conversation doesn't get very far unless we're invited [to discuss their library]."

LSSI argues that it can solve problems such as maintaining service levels on reduced budgets and filling leadership openings because of its corporate resources, size, and expertise. It claims that it can manage a public library on the same budget and still make a profit. "We make only a little on public library contracts," says Dubberly. He maintains that LSSI finds profits by saving money on previous inefficiencies: "I've been a librarian and a library director. . . . I've been on both sides and I can guarantee you that there are inefficiencies in the total system. We just do it leaner."

Although LSSI has no control over the total budget of any public library it manages, it can often exert considerable control over the contract for service, as we see in chapter 2.

NOTES

1. Paul Starr, "The Meaning of Privatization," *Yale Law and Policy Review* 6 (1988): 6–41, www.princeton.edu/~starr/meaning.html. Also, http://en.wikipedia.org/wiki/Privatization.

2. Florida Library Association, "Florida Public Libraries and Privatization: A Guide for Florida Library Boards and Friends," September 2000, www.leg.state.fl.us/publications/2001/house/reports/tourism/lib_pdfs/AppendF.pdf.

3. New Jersey Library Association Executive Board, "Statement on Outsourcing Public Library Services," www.njla.org/statements/outsourcing.pdf.

4. Massachusetts Board of Library Commissions, http://mblc.state.ma.us/advisory/trustees/privatization_pl.pdf.

5. California Library Association, "A Letter to CLA Membership," July 26, 2011, www.cla-net.org/displaycommon.cfm?an=1&subarticlenbr=296.

6. David Streitfeld, "Anger as a Private Company Takes Over Libraries," *New York Times*, September 26, 2010, www.nytimes.com/2010/09/27/business/27libraries.html?_r=2&src=busln.

2
HOW PRIVATIZATION WORKS: RFPS, CONTRACTS, AND DATA ANALYSIS

Although there are no national standards for conducting the privatization process, there are generally accepted principles that focus on protecting the taxpayer when a service is moved from public to private management. State laws in Massachusetts, Florida, and the District of Columbia set forth some criteria:

- Governments should discuss with the community privatization's purpose and values before writing a request for proposal (RFP). Once an RFP is distributed, the validity of privatization becomes an assumption. This discussion should include the problems that lead to privatization and can forestall a public outcry later in the process.
- Governments should ensure that the RFP clearly states the intent of the privatization, outlines the services required of the contractor, and establishes explicit criteria for evaluating RFP responses.
- There should be clear potential for savings without increasing costs to the taxpayer.
- There should be multiple competitors for the contract. Bruce Wallin, describing the history of privatization in Massachusetts, puts it this way: "Moving from a government monopoly to a private sector monopoly is not necessarily an improvement."[1]
- Governments must maintain ultimate control of the services. The contractor must be accountable for performance, and any contract should have performance indicators of quantity, quality, and the results of the service. Governments must hold the contractor responsible for meeting these indicators.
- If the contractor cannot perform the service, governments must plan for a no-risk, low-cost way of returning the service to government management.
- There should be minimal adverse employee impact. Some state laws specify that government employees transferred to private management continue to have pension and health benefits and even a salary competitive with other government workers.

EXAMINATION OF RFPS AND CONTRACTS FOR LIBRARY PRIVATIZATION

Much of this section is based on research done by Heather Hill for her 2009 dissertation, "Outsourcing the Public Library: A Critical Discourse Analysis."[2] Hill reviewed more than thirty documents, including RFPs for library management, the responses, and subsequent contracts, and came to three overarching conclusions:

- The contractor has an enormous amount of power in defining the library for a particular community.
- RFPs are normative. Simply issuing the RFP implies that privatization is an acceptable if not preferable way to manage a library and creates an expectation that a contract for privatization will be written. Once this assumption is made, protests from the library staff, board, or even community are sometimes dismissed as uninformed and reflecting an irrational fear of change.
- Many of the contract management criteria are decided by the contractor after the contract is already in place.

RESPONSES TO THE RFP

Hill found that responses to RFPs were very general. In our own review of six responses to RFPs, we confirmed much of what Hill found. The most detailed sections of these proposals concerned the number of the library's open hours and the number of library employees. There were significant similarities and even repetition among all of LSSI's RFP responses, including description of work performed in other libraries; the processes they would use; and general description of work they would do after the contract was awarded, rather than outcomes they would achieve. For example, the responses indicated that they would

- Establish long- and short-term goals
- Interview, select, and hire qualified staff
- Provide monthly financial statements
- Work closely with the city manager, citizen's advisory group, and related library support groups
- Plan and conduct a comprehensive collection review
- Develop a marketing plan
- Investigate supplemental revenue sources
- Provide a plan for establishing fees and fines
- Establish ILL arrangements
- Maintain required insurance
- Administer a community survey (in one proposal LSSI would charge extra for this)
- Budget and responsibly manage the library's fiscal operations
- Define core library performance measures

These are prospective activities, including the critical definition of core library performance measures. It is the employer that should define and set performance standards; these responses reverse that custom and allow the contractor to define and set how its own performance will be judged. Furthermore, these activities involve additional planning rather than identifying specific improvements or changes in library service.

Although Hill found responses to RFPs to be vague in tangibles promised, our observations found that if the RFP asked for a specific commitment, such as number of hours to be open, the company made the commitment.

To some extent, this pattern of very general responses is a result of very general RFPs. In the four RFPs reviewed, three were almost identical, suggesting that a governing authority minimally customized a document borrowed from a neighboring community. One of these RFPs did, however, state that the contractor would use the state library's benchmark measurements, and that the "contractor's proposal will provide a level of service that is consistent or superior to that currently delivered." The fourth RFP was tailored for the community's libraries, perhaps because of the significant input from three librarians.

THE CONTRACT

The most disturbing aspect of Hill's research was that, in all cases she reviewed, the contract was written from the contractor's point of view and contained almost no performance measures by which to evaluate the implementation of the contract and thus the quality of library service. The contracts were all remarkably similar and included little protection for the governing body regarding the contractor's performance.

Our review of three contracts supports Hill's analysis that the contractor controls the contract process, even though public officials should be setting the terms. Here are some examples of language that favors the contractor:

- Confidentiality of any information that LSSI declares to be confidential, even after the contract ends: "LSSI accepts no responsibility for any lawsuits, claims, demands, that might arise relating to pensions, benefits, or grievances as a result of labor issues arising with the transfer of government employees to a private company."
- Prohibition of the library hiring any LSSI employees for six months after the contract ends: This provision makes it difficult for a governing body ending a contract to hire current employees to continue library service. LSSI did waive this requirement for some libraries whose contract ended amicably.

Hill found little evidence that local governing bodies develop contracts that protect themselves, the library users, or the community. Nearly every contract is clearly provided by or influenced by LSSI and is designed to give the contractor primary control over, not just library functions, but all the strategic plans and operations that feed into library policies and services. As Hill puts it, "In all the contracts, the municipality is looking to the contractor to define the public library in a given time period after the contract is already in place."[3]

IMPLICATIONS

One concern Hill raises is the reliance on model RFPs and contracts to aid governing bodies and library boards in preparing these documents. Our analysis of RFPs and contracts indicates that existing models do not benefit library service. RFP models should not be a cookie-cutter template in which the governing body changes only the name of the community. A better model for both RFPs and contracts is a checklist that indicates the *types* of information a community should include that would direct the contractor to meet that community's specific library needs (see the appendix for one example).

Another issue raised by Hill is that the governing body rarely has the expertise to design an RFP or a contract that describes high-quality library service and specifies performance measurements. In deciding to privatize and thus hire an "expert" in managing libraries, the local government thus relies on the expert to design all plans, strategies, and the contract itself without providing critical input or oversight. Hill goes on to say: "The legitimization of the contractor as an expert places it in a powerful role in defining what library service is and should be. In designating the expert, any who try to challenge the decisions of the expert [e.g., the current library staff] are at a disadvantage because they lack the prestige and the authority to do so.[4]

A third issue raised by Hill is the relationship between policy development and policy approval and the fact that both of these functions take place after the contract is already in place. As Hill puts it:

> Those who plan and create policy documents are much more familiar with the policies' contexts and purposes than a representative . . . of a governmental body whose main priority is probably not the governing of the library. . . . Additionally, the policy plans are not part of the contract. The task to create policies is given in the contracting documents, but the resulting policies are not created until after the contractor assumes responsibility for providing library service; in some cases they are created over the first year of the contract. . . . If the community members or the municipality believes there are significant disagreements or deficiencies with a contractor's policies when they are presented a year after a contract has been in place, there are only two outcomes. Either the municipality satisfactorily rehashes the policies with the contractor or the municipality ends the contract.[5]

A fourth issue is the criteria for performance measurement. Almost no contracts we reviewed had any actual performance measurements. Setting performance expectations for libraries is more complicated than setting those for trash pickup, for example. Either the trash is picked up and disposed of on time or it is not. And if it is not, the local government is quick to hear about it. A multifaceted, complicated service such as a library performance is much harder to measure—particularly for a government body without the specific expertise to do so. However, the government body could specify that the library's performance on state data elements must remain the same or even improve from year to year. This, of course, requires that the body be aware of the data that allow libraries to track their performance over time and to compare their performance to other libraries.

For specific advice on drafting effective, meaningful RFPs and contracts, see chapter 4 and the appendix.

NOTES

1. Bruce A. Wallin, *Privatization of State Services in Massachusetts: Politics, Policy, and an Experiment That Wasn't* (Boston, MA: Department of Political Science, Northeastern University, 1995), 4.

2. Heather Hill, "Outsourcing the Public Library: A Critical Discourse Analysis," Ph.D. diss., Information Science and Learning Technologies, University of Missouri, 2009, https://mospace.umsystem.edu/xmlui/bitstream/handle/10355/6126/research.pdf?sequence=3.

3. Ibid., 108.

4. Ibid., 62.

5. Ibid., 87–88.

3

A CLOSER LOOK AT PRIVATIZATION: FIVE CASE STUDIES

Case studies of a variety of public library systems provide some insight into how the process of privatizing a library takes place and what changes in service, staffing, and environment occur under private management. Two of the libraries studied here are under private management as this book is being produced; one was under private management and reverted back to public management; and two considered privatization but rejected it.[1]

Each case study is based on multiple interviews by the authors and a data comparison which, when relevant, shows basic performance indicators against a comparable library and statewide averages.

STATISTICS USED

Robert Ward's research, published in *Administration and Society* in 2007, provided the guidance for the choice of performance measures in these case studies.[2] Ward chose library visits, items held, items circulated, and reference services. In his study, he looked at seven libraries that had been privatized and evaluated them according to these "economic efficiency" measures. Our survey considers all of Ward's measures except reference services, because the number of reference inquiries have decreased in public libraries nationwide.

Furious debate follows the publication of any work that proposes or uses metrics to identify high-quality public library service. We do not claim to have found the right measures or the right mix of measures to gauge the performance of public libraries, but these are measures that can be used—ideally with a more comprehensive look at a library's unique situation—to understand a library's performance over time or in comparison with similar libraries.

In identifying libraries to compare to privatized libraries, we asked the data coordinators in each state library to help narrow the field of possible comparisons to one specific library. The comparisons in this publication are not provided to demonstrate that one of the libraries is better than the other. Instead, these comparisons give a sense of how each community supports and uses its library and invites closer study of each.

Determining whether private libraries satisfy their community's library needs also requires studies that use qualitative methods. The quality and impact of an individual library's services do not show up in measures, for example, of the number of children's programs or an audience count. The most significant questions include "Are these programs the right ones for the community?" "Are they offered at the best times to meet community needs?" "What are the results of these programs?" Questions such as these, which must be answered to judge a library's success, are beyond this publication's scope.

FINNEY COUNTY PUBLIC LIBRARY

Because of its remote, rural location, the Finney County (Kansas) Public Library had difficulty recruiting and retaining a qualified library director. After several searches during the 1990s, the board of trustees contracted with LSSI to ensure that the library maintained continuous leadership. The library has renewed the contract with LSSI three times and is still privately managed by the company.

Finney County, located in the southwest section of Kansas (approximately 200 miles west of Wichita), is a predominantly agricultural region. Although it is the second largest county in Kansas, covering more than 1,300 square miles, the population is around only 37,000, with a median household income of $44,364.[3]

The Finney County Public Library, located in Garden City, is the only public library serving the county. Its total operating income from local income in FY 2009 was $900,571 and expenditures were $948,054.[4] The majority of the library's funding comes from the county. A board of trustees oversees library operations and has the authority to sign contracts and make budget decisions. Five of the trustees are appointed by the county commission and the sixth is a county commissioner.

Time Line of Privatization

In 2002, although he was not a member of the library's board of trustees at the time, the board's current chairman, Rocky Cook, served on a search committee for a library director. He recalls that during the mid- to late 1990s previous committees had "exhausted themselves" seeking a qualified professional to head the library.

In 2002 the director of the regional library system that advises local libraries in southwest Kansas mentioned LSSI to the search committee; this was the first time the volunteers had heard of the library management company. The committee, thinking that a national contractor might be well suited to solving the problem of recruiting and retaining a qualified library director, brought the idea to the board of trustees.

"The trustees approached LSSI," explains Cook. "They didn't approach us to try to sell themselves to us." During the next few months, the company met with the trustees and made a presentation. "The library requested a quote and asked for guarantees of service, and that initiated the paperwork that followed," recalls Cook. Asked if other companies were invited to bid on library management, he says, "As far as we knew, LSSI was the only one doing this."

The library director search committee took steps to qualify LSSI: "Before we got serious [about a contract], the search committee contacted members of other boards of trustees at libraries managed by LSSI," explains Cook. "We heard their comments—we considered their responses unbiased—and we did not hear one substantially negative comment."

The Contract

Negotiations over the first contract evolved over several months, and LSSI provided initial language for the contract. "I think LSSI presented the initial draft, and that then served as the basis for our negotiation," states Cook.

The board of trustees negotiated several points in that first draft, including staff benefits and capital expenditures. "The trustees were very concerned that the staff not lose their benefits," says Cook. "Some of the staff had worked at the library for a long time, and they [made the transition to working for LSSI] without having a waiting period for their benefits. We scrutinized [the benefits packages] closely. Some things were a little better, some weren't as good, but in the balance it felt pretty equitable for the staff."

According to Erin Francoeur, Finney County's current library director, the majority of staff made the transfer and still work at the library under LSSI. Based on their comments, she says, "Before the contract was put in place, there was a series of meeting with the library staff and the board of trustees, and then with representatives from LSSI. In both cases, staff were allowed to ask questions and give input on what should be included in the contract." Francoeur confirms that many of the staff's county benefits were grandfathered in for those hired by LSSI.

Another issue that the board of trustees wanted changed in the initial draft of the contract was capital expenditures. "The trustees own the library building and everything that's in it," explains Cook. "It wouldn't be appropriate for LSSI to assume major expenses or improvements for that property when it isn't theirs. Maintenance, yes, but not major repairs. So it was a matter of coming to an agreement on where to draw the line."

The three-year contract went into effect in 2003, and when it expired the board of trustees renewed for five years. "However, the contract is reviewed annually and both parties have the option to back out with six months' notice," says Cook. "The board has an agenda item to review it every year. We haven't changed it materially, just reworded sections for clarification."

The library director, and often LSSI's regional director, generally attend monthly board meetings so that issues or questions are dealt with as they arise. "We can ask the regional director how other libraries are handling something," says Cook.

As for annual increases, Cook says, "We've tried to increase our budget for collection expenditures, and [LSSI] has encouraged us to do that. It just depends on our budget."

The current contract with LSSI expires at the end of 2011. "In my opinion, we plan to continue the current arrangement, assuming nothing changes," Cook states. "LSSI is here at our request to carry out our wishes. It is a partnership."

Finney County Contracts

Each of Finney County's contracts states: "LSSI will provide an on-site MLS-degreed and qualified Library Director/Project Manager who has the background and expertise to execute [services outlined in the contract]. The Library Director/Project Manager hired by LSSI shall be assigned to the project at the discretion of the Board of Trustees."

The first contract outlines how all library staff hired by LSSI will begin to receive employee benefits. Details include the transfer of funds invested in the Kansas Public

Employees Retirement System to LSSI's 401(k) plan and a ninety-day grace period for receiving health care benefits from the county. It also states that "LSSI will recognize the length of employment with FCPL of each Library Workforce employee in calculating health care and vacation benefits."

Subsequent contracts and attachments contain little new information. In 2007, however, an "Action Items" section was added that outlines specific plans for the year. The first of these is a 5 percent raise for all LSSI employees working in the Finney County Library, with the stated purpose of making their wages "comparable to that paid by other libraries in the region."

Other staff-related plans outlined for 2007—and repeated verbatim for the next four years—include moving staff from "back-room operations to direct patron service whenever possible"; training staff to "take on a larger role with direct patron assistance"; and increasing diversity, maturity, skill mix, and educational level of staff when possible.

Another section under Action Items for 2007 is facilities. LSSI states that it will help to seek funding for creating a public computer lab in the library, remodeling or refurnishing specific parts of the library, improving lighting, and so forth.

The contracts contain no budget or financial details other than the total operating expense and minimum amount to be spent on library materials—which includes LSSI's handling fee. The contracts each specify that this fee of 5 percent will be "subsumed" in each total monthly payment to LSSI.

Data and Library-to-Library Comparison

From FY 2003 to 2009, the materials held by the Finney County Library decreased by 29.48 percent. The number of items circulated decreased by 9.42 percent. Visits to the library increased by less than 1 percent. During this period, the funds from Finney County's mill levy rose 30.18 percent.

	Finney County Public Library			
FY	**Population Served**	**Materials Held**	**Library Visits**	**Items Lent**
2003	39,732	203,496	223,496	245,360
2009	40,998	143,521	224,472	222,256
Change	3.1%	−29.48%	0.44%	−9.42%

The State Library of Kansas recommended the Hutchinson Public Library as a similar library in Kansas. It serves almost the same population as Finney County's, and each town is home to a community college.

Hutchinson Public Library

FY	Population Served	Materials Held	Library Visits	Items Lent
2003	40,741	286,656	216,112	508,826
2009	40,889	291,109	435,299	438,726
Change	0.36%	1.6 %	101.42%	−13.78%

The following chart compares three service measures from 2009 statistics between the two libraries and Kansas libraries.

Measure, per Capita	Finney County	Hutchinson	Kansas Average
Library Visits	5.48	10.65	6.59
Items Circulated	5.42	10.73	11.86
Materials Held	3.50	6.39	4.87

Effects of Privatization

Contracting with LSSI solved Finney County's ongoing problem of finding a qualified, MLS-degreed library director. Although at least two directors have been hired and then left under LSSI, the company provided interim directors between hires. As Cook points out, "We've had more than one library director [since 2003], but we've never gone without one."

Perhaps simply as a result of ensuring stable management, Cook says, "we have a more productive, better trained, more responsive staff with LSSI. LSSI has helped provide us with a comprehensive program for collection development, and technical assistance for projects like automation planning—which we don't have a great deal of expertise in." He points out that, given the independent status and remote location of Finney County Public Library, "We would have been compelled to bring in outside consultants (outsourcing) to help us with things like automation."

Francoeur says that since 2003 the collection budget has grown from approximately $80,000 to approximately $120,000. "Money that was saved elsewhere goes into our materials budget," she says. "I'd attribute this to LSSI, because they make collection growth a focus. They want libraries to keep their collections up to date and relevant to the community." All selection and purchasing decisions for the collection are done by local staff (who are all LSSI employees), without oversight or requirements from LSSI headquarters.

Cook states that LSSI has met the board's expectations and that the trustees are satisfied with the arrangement. "Now, the board does not have to concern itself with recruiting or retaining [a library director]. We [turned] over the operation and management of the library to LSSI. [The board] wanted to maintain policy and general oversight—but we weren't interested in being directly involved in the day-to-day operations. [Now] we're able to concentrate on strategic planning for the library, capital improvements, and the like."

In Conclusion

Until they contracted with LSSI, Finney County had one difficult issue—finding and keeping a library director—which had a substantial impact on the quality of their library services. The lack of consistent, knowledgeable leadership in a library can impact everything from policy creation to staff morale. LSSI was able to fill that gap (literally) by providing library directors and, perhaps, stability through consistent training and management from its headquarters.

JACKSON-MADISON COUNTY LIBRARY

Located in Jackson, Tennessee, the Jackson-Madison County Library (JMCL) is funded by, and serves, both the city and Madison County. A board of trustees—three of whose members are appointed by the city and four by the county—oversees the library.

In 2006, when the board decided to seek private management for the library, the Madison County Commission sued on the grounds that the board did not have the right to do so. The board won the case and an ensuing appeal. Before the last lawsuit was settled, they had contracted with LSSI to run the library beginning in November 2006.

Madison County, population 98,294, is located in west Tennessee; its county seat is Jackson. The 2009 U.S. Census shows that the county has a median household income of $54,990.[5] The county's economy is based primarily on educational, health, and social services, manufacturing, and retail trade.[6]

In FY 2008/9, JMCL received $1,024,600 for its operating budget, and its expenditures were $1,014,567. The library is funded through taxes collected by the county and by the City of Jackson. Starting July 1, 2011, the library closed on Sundays due to a $60,000 decrease in funding provided by Madison County.

Time Line of Privatization

The JMCL board of trustees conducted its search for a private management company in 2006 after finalizing its decision in a January 2006 meeting, with then-JMCL executive director Thomas Aud present. Aud says the board voted to seek private management companies in an executive session, with only voting board members present and no minutes recorded.

Asked why the board initially considered a change to private management, Sharon Younger, a member of the board of trustees from 2006 to 2011, explains: "It was a whole bundle of things. Year over year, utilization of the library was trending down, both in circulation and in number of visits. We were also under pressure financially, and were afraid that we'd have to lay people off. The library . . . was seeing only minor funding increases each year. Meanwhile, personnel costs went up every year."

Younger recalls that the board of trustees drafted an RFP for library management services and posted it publicly through ALA and perhaps other sources. She says that board members were aware that LSSI was managing three public library systems in neighboring Shelby County, but the board did not approach LSSI directly. "Board members visited those libraries" during the RFP process, states Younger. Representatives of those libraries "had nothing but good things to say about LSSI; that made us feel it was worthwhile to pursue."

At the January 2006 meeting, the board offered Aud the opportunity to have the library staff respond to the RFP. JMCL staff did submit a proposal, as did Information International Associates (IIA) and LSSI. Because the library staff was a competitor in the process, they did not provide input on the RFP or contract—although the board asked them to submit current library data for the RFP.

Younger explains: "In the RFP, we had set parameters for the percentage of budget to be spent on books, the number of MLS librarians on board—that type of thing. We evaluated the proposals on how well they met those parameters and then went through an interview process to get a better feel for each of them."

The three respondents also presented their proposals at a public hearing on October 4. "At the public hearing, we each got to make a presentation in a set amount of time," explains Aud. "We went first, then IIA, and then LSSI. LSSI took longer; they were given extra time by the board."

Aud estimates that one hundred to one hundred and fifty people attended the public hearing, most of them against privatizing the library. Petitions against privatizing—or against making any decision without more public input—had been circulated and turned in to the board, but these actions did not stop the process.

Aud pointed out that one specific request in the RFP was to specify the management fee that would be included in the budget. "Of course, we would not charge an additional fee, and we said so in our proposal," Aud says. "When I saw LSSI's proposal, they had refused to answer that question, and even stated at [the public hearing] that they were a private company and so did not have to answer the question."

Regarding the board's selection of LSSI, Younger says, "The library staff didn't really come back with what we considered to be a proposal. They gave us more of a presentation of the status quo." As for IIA, which had not managed any public libraries, Younger says simply, "We felt LSSI had a more aggressive plan for meeting our requirements." Aud commented, "I think they had already made up their minds [back in January]."

The Initial Contract

"We hired a law firm to draw up a contract for us, and we sent it to LSSI," says Younger. "Then we, our lawyers, and LSSI went back and forth with it." She doesn't recall any negotiations over content but says, "We wanted to keep the lines very clear. Tennessee law says that the board is responsible for hiring the library director. Even though that person would be an employee of LSSI, we wanted to make sure we made the hiring decision."

In the subsequent contract (covering November 2009 to November 2011), the board made no changes; because funding remained flat, the budget did not increase.

RFP, Proposal, and Contracts

JMCL's contract with LSSI is based on both the RFP and LSSI's response and specifically refers to these documents as containing the desired services from the contractor. The contract also bases financial information on cost data included in the proposal. When the county and city renewed the contract in 2009, the contract again included the RFP and the LSSI proposal.

The 42-page LSSI proposal covers library services extensively but lacks specifics regarding hard deliverables. For example, the proposal promises to assess the current state of the library and then, based on that assessment, set long- and short-term goals for indicators including circulation, number of visits, and the like. The section on a library staffing plan, on the other hand, is very precise.

The lack of performance measures is initially the fault of the RFP, which required respondents to demonstrate competencies in a number of core management areas including performance measures and reporting but then failed to require the responders to address them. Furthermore, the city and the county did not set performance measures or a method to evaluate them in subsequent contracts.

Data and Library-to-Library Comparison

In the first two years under private management, JMCL nearly doubled the amount spent on collection materials, resulting in a substantial increase in materials held and in library visits. The growth in visits might also be attributed to the increased number of the library's public access computers.

	Jackson-Madison County Library			
FY	**Population Served**	**Materials Held**	**Library Visits**	**Items Lent**
2005/6	94,397	163,616	168,000	205,618
2008/9	96,376	181,850	274,500	250,076
Change	2.10%	11.14%	63.39%	21.62%

Cleveland Bradley County Public Library (CBCPL), a library that is comparable to JMCL in population, saw a 32 percent reduction in its materials budget for FY 2008/9 yet still managed to increase the number of materials held and general circulation—to a lesser extent than JMCL, but greatly exceeding JMCL's (by more than 100,000) at a time when it was spending $44,000 less on materials.

Cleveland Bradley County Library

FY	Population Served	Materials Held	Library Visits	Items Lent
2005/6	91,196	159,886	239,067	326,827
2008/9	96,472	188,244	282,718	356,050
Change	5.47%	15.06%	15.44%	8.21%

In fact, CBCPL exceeds JMCL on per capita measures including library visits, items lent, number of borrowers, and items held. This may be attributed to the fact that JMCL is still building an up-to-date, comprehensive collection after years of insufficient funding. Younger says, "We figure it will take us fifteen more years to get the collection to where it should be."

The following chart compares three service measures from the FY 2008/9 statistics from the two libraries and Tennessee averages.

Measure, per Capita	Jackson-Madison County	Cleveland Bradley County	Tennessee Average
Library Visits	2.85	2.93	3.51
Items Circulated	2.59	3.69	4.07
Materials Held	1.89	1.95	2.21

Effects of Privatization

There were many changes at JMCL after privatization, many of them specifically dictated by the contract. The library added Sunday hours and opened a long-wished-for branch library in December 2008 (with no additional funding).

Younger believes that the main difference in the library under private management is the growth and updating of the collection: "The main problem was that we didn't have any new books or materials. Before LSSI came in, 7 or 8 percent of the budget was going to [collection development]. Our contract with LSSI required that 20 percent of the budget be spent on new books and materials." In addition, JMCL received a $250,000 grant eighteen months prior to the changeover, which the library used for purchasing new materials. "We want to keep the focus on new materials coming in," says Younger. LSSI also performed some much-needed weeding of obsolete and damaged materials to make more room for the larger collection.

LSSI improved and expanded the public access computers in JMCL as well, using grant money and other funding sources to add computers and move stations into the lobby of the main library. "Under LSSI, we were able to increase our [twelve to fifteen] public access computers by about 50 percent," says library director Richard Salmons. "We're modernizing all of them, gradually."

Library staffing today remains approximately the same as before the contract, even with the branch library. Salmons says eight of his eighteen FTE staff members worked under public management; five others were hired by LSSI and have since retired. Aud points out that when hours were reduced in 2011 some full-time staff had their hours reduced but reportedly retained full-time benefits. A strong volunteer program supplements staffing.

One unforeseen effect of privatizing arose in 2011, when it was discovered that, once the initial contract began, the library had stopped contributing to the state pension for retired and former employees. That money for pensions had traditionally come out of the library's operations budget but was never included in the RFP, contract, or subsequent budgets. The city and county were forced to contribute $60,000 each to make up for the missed payments. The city did so, but the county, perhaps still smarting from losing the lawsuits, indicated that its share must come out of the library budget. Hence, the $60,000 shortfall and reduction in service hours and staffing hours. (The county has not increased its funding to the library since before the privatization debate began.)

Comments and Advice

The sources interviewed for this case study offered advice to similar libraries that might be considering privatizing their library management. Thomas Aud had this to say: "Look closely at why such a change is being considered. Is it financial, political, or else? Who is driving the process? Is the board doing its 'due diligence' in looking at all aspects before pursuing such a change?" And, given JMCL's tug-of-war between the library board and the county, "Is it legal for your community to do so? Who has the authority: the board of trustees only, the board with the funding government(s), the funding government only?" Aud also recommends that others ask, "Will the library and the community be improved that dramatically by such a change? Would a change of library director and/or some library staff or other changes be possible within the public sector to accomplish desired results? What does the community want from their public library?"

"I recommend the RFP process," Sharon Younger concludes. "It's a good way to vet everything on the front end. And I like the contract that we negotiated with LSSI. I'd be happy to offer it up to other [library boards] to work from." She adds, "LSSI has been a valuable partner for us. They are not a problem—our biggest problem has been getting funding. We're under constant threat of having funding cut. But LSSI has stuck with us. Of course, the contract states that they have to run the library for the amount of money that we have."

Richard Salmons says, "Be open-minded, and don't listen to half-truths. Before you pass judgment, take a look at the reality; if you have the opportunity, talk to current LSSI directors."

In Conclusion

With the state of local politics complicating the environment and funding of JMCL, LSSI and the board of trustees have a "tough row to hoe." Unless funding increases, the improvements made under private management will slow or even stop. And, as we are preparing this book, JMCL's private management is again coming under fire by the county commission, due to the pension funding snafu.

CALABASAS PUBLIC LIBRARY

The City of Calabasas privatized the management of its public library for approximately nine years, from July 1998 through 2006. The city contracted with a private company to handle library operations from the time Calabasas left the county library system and instituted an independent municipal library. When the third three-year contract ended, the city took over management of the library.

Calabasas, located in Southern California's Los Angeles County, is a relatively new city; it was incorporated in 1991. The city has approximately 23,058 residents, and in 2009 the estimated median household income was $116,761.[7]

Until 1998, the Calabasas library was a part of the County of Los Angeles Public Library (LACPL). A small LACPL branch served the community. Once the city established an independent municipal library, it grew steadily until today Calabasas Public Library is housed in its city-owned, 27,000-square-foot building and serves 31,047 borrowers. The library's total operating income for FY 2009/10 was $1,476,325, with total expenditures of $1,325,864.[8]

Time Line of Privatization

The city's decision to outsource library management came about because the city council no longer wanted Los Angeles County to provide library services to their community. They were unhappy with the quality of service their community was receiving and when, in 1994, California state legislation passed that allowed libraries to split off from larger systems, this made their decision possible.

Ellen Pangarliotas, one of the city's founding mothers and then a member of the parks and recreation commission, had estimated that Calabasas residents paid more than $500,000 each year in property taxes for the library services they received, and that those same services cost the county only $263,000. The city's LACPL branch library was a single 1,400-square-foot room in a shopping center. Margaret Donnellan Todd, current LACPL director, explains that 1998 was a very difficult financial time for the library system, which had lost 50 percent of its funding and so had to cut services. "There was not much that the county could have done," she says.

Throughout 1996 and 1997, Pangarliotas repeatedly urged the city manager to withdraw Calabasas from LACPL and use the city's tax money to set up an independent municipal public library. After more than a year, the council formed a task force to review the idea. A feasibility study showed that Calabasas could easily support an independent library. At the end of 1997, the city council formally alerted the county that the city would be withdrawing from its library system, and then it did withdraw, with the assistance of legal counsel.

Members of the city council understood that the new entity would basically be starting from scratch, because the county system owned almost all the library's assets. The new library would start with no collection to speak of, no furniture or equipment, no staff—and no council members with any library experience. Under these circumstances, the city council opted to contract out the library management to a private firm.

In 1997 this type of contract was relatively new territory. Pangarliotas happened to read an article in the *Los Angeles Times* about neighboring Riverside County, which had outsourced the management of its libraries to LSSI. She set up a meeting with her city manager and representatives from LSSI, and soon afterward the council voted to award a three-year contract to the company.

At that time, Pangarliotas explains, "LSSI was the only game in town." Therefore, the city council did not request multiple bids on the library contract. Robin Parker, director of administrative services for the City of Calabasas, was city clerk at the time. She confirms, "At that time, the task force and our consultants could not find any other companies with the capabilities to meet our needs."

The city's branch library closed on June 30, 1998, and reopened two weeks later under LSSI's management. Between April 16, 1998, when the contract was signed, and mid-July, LSSI helped the city purchase and process an "opening day" collection for a total cost of $225,000 (selected by a board of librarians within LSSI); hired and trained new staff members; installed a new computer system; and provided equipment, supplies, and furnishings. Pangarliotas recalls that the owners of LSSI, Frank and Judy Pezzanite, and their three teenage children came from Maryland to help stock shelves and make sure the library was ready to open.

LSSI also helped the city develop new policies and procedures for the library, and the city took steps to form its first library commission.

Over the next nine years, the Calabasas library grew its collection, its services, its programming, and its hours and outgrew its space three times. Ultimately, the library moved into its own building—thanks in great part to an $8.2 million grant from the state. The library director hired by LSSI contributed significantly to drafting the grant proposal.

In 2007, when the third consecutive contract with LSSI expired, the library reverted to city management. "We had always planned on bringing the library back in house," explains Parker. "We prefer to retain control—that's why [the city originally] split from the county."

Parker and Pangarliotas describe the transition from private to public management as "seamless." Parker estimates that the city is saving $65,000 a year by bringing management in-house. "We didn't save a whole lot of money, when you consider our total budget," she points out.

The Contract

In March 1998, LSSI submitted a proposal that served as a guideline for the city to set up the new municipal library. According to Parker, the proposal advised the city on how to withdraw and start an independent library and included options for staffing and hours, automation systems, and acquisitions expenditures.

The final, approved contract covered three years and followed that proposal very closely. "At first," says Pangarliotas, "we were almost on a month-to-month contract. We made it clear that the plan was always that the library would eventually be city-run—we just didn't know how long that would take." One official change was made to the contract in September 1999, expanding the hours of the library from 45 to 52 hours a week.

Parker says of the first contract, "We negotiated some things, such as hours, [automation] systems, and so forth. We had a very strong task force that knew what they wanted. Ultimately, we were very happy with [the final contract]." The pricing set forth in the proposal did not change substantially in the final contract.

The contract does not mention library policy, and Pangarliotas recalls that the city and LSSI worked closely together on policies. The library commission controlled the library's budget and policies.

Barbara Lockwood, who was hired by LSSI in 1998 as a part-time children's librarian, is now library director at Calabasas Public Library. She explains that all collection decisions were made by the on-site librarians—who were LSSI employees—without "corporate" input: "We selected everything in the collection; LSSI set us up with vendors and we ordered everything. We didn't need to get approval on collection purchases." Lockwood also says that the library's hours, programs, and services were all dictated by the needs of the community. Again, the local librarians had free rein, as long as they stayed within budget constraints.

Pangarliotas says that "every year, [LSSI] asked for a 5 percent increase, at most, and they always told us what it would be used for."

Unlike other management contracts reviewed here, all Calabasas contracts specified amounts that LSSI must spend for each of the contract's three years for staffing (and outlined levels of staffing), automation services, collection development, and general office expenses. The first contract included requirements for planning and funding for a stand-alone automation system as well as purchasing, cataloging, and processing an "opening-day collection" of 14,000 titles. It also detailed staffing requirements as 6.5 FTE employees, offering 45 hours of service per week.

Subsequent contracts included a collection development note: "LSSI will administer the materials budget appropriated by the City [amount not mentioned or included in outlined costs]. LSSI will charge a handling fee of 7.5% on all collection resources purchased or licensed for the library."

Data and Library-to-Library Comparison

Because Calabasas Public Library was under private management for nearly nine years, it makes little sense to track the differences before and after. Here, instead, is a snapshot of the library in FY 2010 along with the same data for a comparable California library, Rancho Mirage Public Library. The latter serves a similar-size population and was also previously a part of a larger county system. The estimated median household income in Rancho Mirage in 2009 was, however, $68,371, considerably lower than that in Calabasas.

	Population Served	Materials Held	Library Visits	Items Lent	Per Capita Collection Expenditures	Total Staff
Calabasas	23,788	58,923	211,360	217,991	$ 5.85	14
Rancho Mirage	22,152	103,618	358,165	622,148	$19.34	23

Although Calabasas has been steadily building its collection for twelve years, it is still nowhere near matching its comparable neighbor. The per capita spending on collection reveals that perhaps the capital costs of getting the Calabasas library up and running diverted funds from materials. According to the latest statistic, Calabasas spends 10 percent less on employee costs than Rancho Mirage but 10 percent more in "other operating expenses." The huge gap in number of items lent in the two communities is telling also. While Calabasas is happy with its new library building and burgeoning collection, Rancho Mirage borrowers are borrowing nearly triple the amount of materials.

The following chart compares three service measures from 2010 statistics for the two libraries and California's libraries.

Measure, per Capita	Calabasas	Rancho Mirage	California Average
Library Visits	8.89	16.17	4.40
Items Lent	9.16	28.09	6.29
Materials Held	2.48	4.67	2.15

Effects of Privatization

The effects of privatizing the library management in Calabasas are difficult to gauge. The fact that the municipal-run library was brand new and benefited tremendously from receiving 100 percent of tax revenues allocated, as opposed to paying into LACPL, muddies the waters of how much of the growth and success can be attributed to out-sourcing versus a change in management. The library's funding was so greatly increased, according to Parker, that even though LSSI was making a profit on the contract, "We still came in at less than our allocated funds for the library. That's how we reserved [funds] for a new library building."

Comments and Advice

Robin Parker reflects, "It all depends on each library's situation—their citizens, what they want to do. If you're looking to save large amounts of money, this is not necessarily a good solution. But if you need new knowledge that you don't have, or are looking for staff or other resources, this would work for you."

Barbara Lockwood recalls her initial position as an LSSI-employed librarian: "There was one thing I always felt conflicted about. LSSI was kind of a distant company, and yet I didn't feel connected to the city administrators either. That may sound crazy—for some time, we were in the same building. But I think the best thing might be to have the library director work for the city, and have LSSI report to that director. All the other employees could work directly for LSSI—but I think the best way to do it is probably to have [the director as] a direct report to the city administration, and the city would have someone in the library who knows how the library works."

In Conclusion

Relying on a private company to provide public library expertise and guidance—and to fulfill library management—was the means by which the City of Calabasas established an independent municipal library. LSSI helped the city succeed in creating a public library that was appropriate for the community's needs, and city administrators were extremely pleased with and grateful to the company.

Part of the success of this business partnership was the fact that the city administrators and the librarians hired by LSSI valued autonomy. Once the new library was up and running, the hands-off management style by the company's corporate headquarters was generally welcomed, and the success of the library relied on the judgment and skills of the local staff.

DARTMOUTH PUBLIC LIBRARIES

Dartmouth is located in southeastern Massachusetts' Bristol County, on land purchased by elders of the Plymouth Colony, and was officially incorporated in 1664. The city had approximately 34,420 residents in 2009, when the median household income was $50,221.[9]

Dartmouth Public Libraries has offered public library services since 1895. The library currently offers services to 14,145 registered borrowers at two buildings, the North Dartmouth Library and the Southworth Library. The library's total operating income for FY 2009/10 was $987,854, with total expenditures of $922,411.[10]

Time Line for the Consideration of Privatization

Previously a prosperous community, Dartmouth faced a budget crunch in 2007 and 2008. In addition to making budget cuts, the city select board examined whether outsourcing some services would save money and preserve jeopardized town services. To investigate possible areas of outsourcing, the selectmen formed the Privatization Study Group.

According to Frank Gracie, who chaired the study group, the group's members reviewed fifteen different town services before deciding to focus on only a few, including trash pickup, school services, and the Department of Public Works (DPW). However, after talking to members of these departments, the group decided not to pursue privatization of these services. Finally, they decided to research outsourcing management of the public library. Gracie had read an article in the *Boston Globe* about LSSI and contacted the company for more information: "I felt privatization was one possible solution to the town's and the library's budget problems. I felt an RFP would bring in detailed information for the library board to make a decision."

The study group prepared a report that focused entirely on the possibility of library management outsourcing, even though they had not discussed the issue with the library director or board. The report prominently mentioned LSSI as a possible contractor and included the FAQ from LSSI about the benefits of their service to the town and even a sample RFP that could be issued.

The Dartmouth Public Libraries' board of trustees is an elected body and thus, despite the interest of the town select board and the town's finance committee, has the final authority to issue an RFP and decide whether to privatize. The study group's report strongly recommended that the library board issue an RFP to gather more information.

The report, which was presented to the select board on April 28, 2008, contained several reasons for considering outsourcing of the library and observed that "a library service is important, but will always be less important than things like the Police and the DPW when tough financial decisions have to be made." LSSI company officials told Gracie they thought they could cut the library's budget from $1 million to $600,000 by making the library more efficient, by automating many services, and by reducing the number of staff.

When the study group presented their recommendations to the select board, they did not release their report to the public in advance of this meeting. By chance, Denise Mederios, the library director at the time, attended the meeting. She says that the study group did not seek information from her or from the library board before preparing and presenting their report.

Gracie believes that the selectmen's personal opinions were divided about privatization but that they would have issued an RFP if they had the authority.

Gracie subsequently made a presentation to the town finance committee, which administers the town's reserve fund. The local newspaper, the *Chronicle*, reported that the finance committee urged library trustees "to draft a Request for Proposal for firms interested in taking over the town's public library." In response to the potential cuts in staff, finance committee member Greg Lyman was quoted in the *Chronicle* as saying, "It really comes down to salaries. . . . Those are the costs that add up and costs so much."

Gracie also presented his report to the library board, which responded negatively to the idea of privatization. Some of the board's concerns were the potential loss of state certification, letting go of union employees, and their belief that the board should and could solve the library's funding problems.

In response to the study group's report, Mederios prepared the Privatization/Outsourcing Report to counter its claims about the benefits of library private management. The library board also asked for information on the financial implications of moving to private management. In her report, Mederios stated that the library was already saving money through outsourcing agreements for several library functions and through cooperative agreements with other libraries such as the SAILS network. (This was of particular concern because SAILS runs the libraries' circulation system and online catalog, allowing reciprocal borrowing among member libraries and handling interlibrary loan.) The Privatization/Outsourcing Report made the point that there was only one company offering private management services and that "contracting to a monopoly provider is unlikely to be an improvement over government service." The report contained detail on the excessive cost to the library of withdrawing from some of its current cooperative arrangements and stated that the Friends group and the Library Foundation had indicated they would stop donating to the library if it was privatized.

Mederios also included the criteria in Massachusetts state law governing privatization, which requires local government to consider (1) need for a competitive marketplace; (2) minimal risk to the public service being privatized; (3) choosing services without legal, political, or practical barriers; and (4) choosing services with minimal adverse employee impact. She felt that contracting with LSSI to manage the library would violate all of these criteria.

In her report, Mederios makes the following points, most in one section of the report, "Direct Responses to Privatization Study Group Report":

- The only data that support the proposition that LSSI saves on the library budget come from LSSI, not from an impartial or a competitive source.
- The library is already fully automated, and a cooperative agreement with the SAILS Library Network would cost $200,000 if Dartmouth Libraries chose to withdraw.
- Ending union contracts would cost $263,000 to pay employees for vacation, sick leave, and unemployment insurance.
- Massachusetts library law requires that local communities "maintain the support" of the local library and must obtain a waiver if funding is not maintained. Though the DPL had requested and received a waiver in the past, a reduction as large as that proposed by outsourcing full management would be a serious impediment to future waivers.
- There would be possible loss of reciprocal borrowing privileges with neighboring communities.
- The American Library Association affirms that publicly funded libraries should remain directly accountable to the public they serve.

The study group report's assertion that the library was less important than police and DPW services was of particular concern to the library board and a probable key factor in the board's decision not to issue an RFP. Mederios described the value of a library to its community: "The Board of Library Trustees feels strongly that public libraries are as important as the Police and DPW. Libraries build communities, foster civic engagement, engage citizens in public decision-making, and transform communities and lives." At a December 2008 board meeting, the board cited many points from Mederios's report and issued a statement that it would not pursue privatization of the library.

In a *Chronicle* article, then library board chair Kathy Murphy-Aisenberg said, "At the library, we're not broken. Our position is that we as a board can run the libraries." The board was also concerned about "eliminating all union jobs" and that outsourcing would negatively affect the quality of the library's staff. The library's union president also suggested that the union might consider taking legal action. Murphy-Aisenberg also said that the library trustees were "not afraid to cut costs every year."

The Outcome

The discussion about privatization/outsourcing the Dartmouth Public Libraries was covered in the local newspapers. Some coverage was neutral, but two editorials strongly opposed privatization. No major public outcry emerged against privatization, most likely because the board made a swift decision to not pursue an RFP.

The budget problems of the town and library continued. In 2009 the town predicted an $800,000 deficit; one action it took to mitigate the deficit was to not renew the town manager's contract. The select board and the finance committee asked the library to contribute to the deficit's reduction by enacting a 15 percent budget cut, thus forcing the library to consider cuts of approximately $150,000. The two bodies had expressed particular concern about the high cost of salaries of library staff, although an editorial in the *Chronicle* pointed out that only 11 percent of the twenty-eight library staff had salaries over $50,000, while at the DPW 34 percent of the "predominantly male" staff of ninety-five had salaries in that range.

The library board considered multiple methods of cutting the budget. The choices came down to reducing youth services, reducing the janitor to half time, and cutting the collection budget or laying off higher paid staff. The board chose to not renew the library director's contract and to keep the position open for a year. When the assistant director, a member of the government workers union, declined to move into the director position, the board eliminated the assistant director position, reduced this position to a senior librarian position, and created a library director position at a lower salary. They also made greater use of volunteers.

Final Comments

In Frank Gracie's view, privatization was a viable option to solve the library's budget problems and should be further evaluated: "The best way to get the specific information needed for the decision process is to initiate an RFP. This gives a clear definition about what the town expects for a service, as well as what a company bids for that service. This takes the guesswork out of the equation and makes things official. *Then* real data can be considered about whether it is the correct path to take for the community. An RFP is nonbinding in the sense that you can dismiss all the bids, but it is binding if you accept a bid which then becomes a contract. It is really a no-lose exercise."

Denise Mederios also considers it important to get accurate information about private management, but this should include information about the full impact on the library. "My report gave the board information to take a stand," she says. She was also concerned that only one company provided these services, stating, "If there is no competition, LSSI is still a monopoly." She went on to say, "I don't think the final goal was to privatize the library. I think it was just to put pressure on the library board to cut the budget . . . and [now] there is a caution about speaking out by the library staff." It is true that the current acting library director and the current library board chair declined to be interviewed for this case study.

In Conclusion

In seeking ways to trim the budget, Dartmouth town leaders were drawn to the seemingly simple solution of privatizing the public library system. Selectmen and committee members with no direct library experience reviewed information provided by the only viable vendor and saw no red flags. When presented with a strong suggestion to seek private management, the library fought back with new facts and arguments. Its report rebutting the benefits of privatization, combined with a library board that quickly and consistently resisted the pressure from its funding bodies, resulted in the quick rejection of the idea.

BEDFORD PUBLIC LIBRARY

Bedford is a suburban city in Tarrant County, Texas, 17 miles northeast of Fort Worth. The projected population in 2008 was 53,937, and in 2009 the median household income was $59,386.[11]

The Bedford Public Library has offered library services since 1964 and currently provides services to 33,762 registered borrowers. The library's total operating income for 2008 was $1,145,073, with total expenditures of $1,030,329.[12]

In 2001 the voters of Bedford passed a bond issue authorizing the city council to issue bonds worth $8 million to build a new library; however, because of the general financial situation in the area, the city council never issued these bonds. In 2004 the city council adopted a tax rate higher than that recommended by the city manager, who had suggested splitting the rate increase over two years. The manager recognized that a tax rate increase greater than 8 percent above the prior year's level would allow residents to petition for an election calling for a vote on a tax rollback. Petitioners gathered enough signatures, and the rollback election was held in March 2005. The rollback provision passed by only ten votes and forced the city to return the tax rate to the prior year's rate, forcing the city to implement budget cuts and layoffs.

The council closed several services, including the city's swimming pools, the recreational center, and the city library, which closed on March 30, 2005. According to ALA,

Bedford was the first U.S. library to close since 1989. The Bedford Friends of the Library and other supporters including a local insurance company raised enough funds to open the library for 21 hours a week. The Friends group continued to raise money until, by October 2005, the library was open 40 hours a week.

Time Line for Consideration of Privatization

In October 2005, members of the Bedford city council attended the Texas Municipal League Conference, where they spoke with an LSSI representative about the Bedford library's financial problems. This conversation resulted in an invitation to LSSI to visit Bedford and its library.

Over the next year, the city council formed an outsourcing committee to review privatizing the library. This committee operated in a transparent manner, and the library board and employees were well aware of their efforts. The city council hired Maria Redburn as library director, who was also aware that the council was considering privatization.

The library board, in private discussions, opposed the concept of privatization from the beginning and in an initial vote on November 15, 2006, voted unanimously against pursuing private management. Redburn says the board stated the following reasons for their opposition:

- concerns about quality of service
- material purchases coordinated by someone in another state and based on current popularity rather than community needs and requests
- loss of control to a for-profit company that did not have to comply with open-records requests
- sending Bedford's tax dollars out of state
- problems reestablishing the library as a city department if the out-sourcing arrangement failed
- laying off employees or reducing their hours despite the loyalty they showed by returning to work after the library reopened in 2005

On November 30, 2006, the city council hosted a public forum on privatizing the library. Representatives from the library board, LSSI, and more than one hundred Bedford residents attended the meeting. LSSI made a presentation about its services and answered questions. Twenty-five Bedford residents testified, almost all opposed to private management. According to the meeting minutes, among other things they asked, "How does LSSI plan to decrease staff and increase hours and services, yet save the city money?" "What is the percentage LSSI will profit?" They also expressed concerns about accountability and sending city money out of state. Many worried that the quality of service from the library would decrease significantly.

During this time, Ralph Chaney was elected chair of the Bedford board of trustees. He says, "I used the power of the position to lobby hard against LSSI. By now, the community was aware what was going on. Neighbors lobbied neighbors. Homeowner groups voiced opposition." Chaney also reminded people that the community had passed a bond issue for a new library in 2001. Redburn says, "The people wanted a new library. They had voted in 2001 to build a new library and nothing had happened. They didn't get a new library they had voted for and instead the city closed it and now is going to outsource staff." The Friends held a petition drive that collected sixteen hundred signatures in three days.

Less than a month after the meeting, in December 2006, the library board took an official position against privatizing the library:

> After extensive research into public library experiences with outsourced management, as well as into LSSI, the Library Board is going on record tonight as unanimously opposing any action by Bedford's City Council to outsource management of the Bedford Public Library. In addition, our Board is convinced that LSSI cannot save the city a worthwhile amount of money and still provide the level of service, selection of materials, and personal service that Bedford residents want and are accustomed to receiving from their local library. The Bedford Library Board believes that retaining the value of the city as a community should be a high priority for council concern.

Despite the strong opposition from the library board and from many residents, the city council continued to investigate privatization and issued an RFP. Members of the library board with library experience helped develop the document, because they wanted to ensure that it included specifics about the level and quality of needed services and measureable benchmarks. Thus, Bedford's RFP was the most detailed of any that we examined.

Even before the council developed the RFP, Redburn, on the advice of a local consultant, prepared a 150-page library business plan, which prepared the library to respond to the RFP. Redburn explains: "Everybody was interested in what the library was doing. People read the business plan and went to the city council meetings and quoted it. When a newspaper article said the library was 'grossly inefficient,' people looked at the business plan and concluded this was not true. The library didn't have to defend itself because people were quoting the plan."

In June 2007, the city council agreed that the library could also submit a response to the RFP to allow for competition. To prepare the proposal, Redburn reviewed similar libraries operated by LSSI and compared them to Bedford. She submitted open public records requests to obtain LSSI documents about these libraries. Redburn used two strategies in her proposal. First, she provided a detailed response to each criterion in the RFP, using both statistical information about the library's performance and heartfelt anecdotes from library users about how they valued the library. The second strategy was to answer specific issues raised by council, such as their request for the library to be open seven days a week. Initially, Redburn's response had been "Give us more money and we will do this." In her proposal, she found a way to reorganize employee hours to open the library on Sundays.

Redburn recalls: "The RFP made us very creative. We felt challenged to think outside the box. . . . We will show them what we can do. No private company is going to run this library better than I can. I looked at every LSSI claim and responded. Seven days a week? We can do that. More materials for less money? We can renegotiate our contracts with vendors. More innovative? We can do new things and get awards. We went on the offensive and applied for every award we could find. We did not act like victims or that we were getting a raw deal. We may have felt like that but we didn't act that way. We knew LSSI always comes in $100,000 cheaper. We decided not to try and match them on money and cut staff. If it comes down to the price, then LSSI is welcome to the library. We focused on quality service, not lower standards."

Redburn also gave clear instructions to library employees not to comment on the privatization issue. She felt it was not her role or that of library employees to incite the public against the city council. "That inflames the situation and could backfire," she explains. The community elects the council and the library board reports to the council, and Redburn thought they needed to maintain good relations. The Friends of the Library and the library board, however, were vocal opponents of privatization.

The city issued the RFP on July 1, 2007, with an August deadline for proposals. According to Redburn, "The city didn't try to be underhanded. They were open about looking at outsourcing." The city received two proposals, one from LSSI and one from the Bedford Public Library.

The Outcome

The city council was closely divided about privatization, with three members strongly in favor of private management and three strongly opposed. The seventh council member, an engineer, was undecided. To reach a decision, this member asked both the library and LSSI to obtain the best price for the same three books that he chose. When the library demonstrated that its cost to order, process, and catalog was cheaper than LSSI's costs by $0.86, the council member voted against privatization and to keep the library under city management.

The community's emotional involvement in the privatization issue returned attention to the bond issue that had never been implemented. Asked what has changed at the library, Chaney says, "Everything changed. As soon as the issue died, I pushed the city to take action on a new library that voters had approved in 2001 as part of a bond package." Rather than build a new library, the city council purchased an abandoned 40,000-square-foot grocery store. "Public meetings were held to get citizen input . . . and even design the library. Teenagers contributed innovative ideas that were used," states Chaney. He believes that the privatization discussion brought the community together around the library: "People who had never had any interest before became a spokesperson" for the library. "The community has a love affair going because the new library really is a community meeting place with local control."

Final Comments

When asked what advice she would give to other libraries, Maria Redburn said, "Take the emotion out of it. We can be passionate about what we do but our passion is sometimes viewed as weakness. We need to be businesslike in our demeanor." She continued, "Have information before they ask for it. Governing bodies don't have much sympathy for government workers who complain. Think of it as business and not personal. Think clearly about what to say and how to present the facts."

When Ralph Chaney was asked what advice he would give, he said, "I would encourage library boards to keep priorities established. Use the power of community forums. Establish community priorities. Collect statistical data on library usage, public usage, student usage, and programs for the community. Visit libraries that are privatized and talk to patrons and staff at those libraries. Meet with council representatives in small group settings." He concluded, "Most of all, make sure the front porch of the library is neat and tidy. Continually strive to be the most attractive and enticing public building."

In Conclusion

Several actions emerge as key factors in the Bedford city council's decision not to privatize the public library. For one, the library was prepared with information about its performance in comparison with other libraries, particularly privatized libraries. Additionally, the long time line in which privatization was discussed allowed the library to prepare an extensive business plan and a response to the RFP. Finally, although the library staff stayed silent, the library board and the Friends of the Library were vocal opponents to privatization and mobilized public opinion against it.

NOTES

1. Interview requests for the following libraries were declined: Bee Cave (Texas) Public Library, Jackson County (Oregon) Public Library, and Moorpark City (California) Library.

2. R. C. Ward, "The Outsourcing of Public Library Management: An Analysis of the Application of New Public Management Theories from the Principal-Agent Perspective," *Administration and Society* 38 (2007): 627–648.

3. U.S. Census Bureau, State and County Quickfacts, http://quickfacts.census.gov/qfd/states/20/20055.html.

4. State Library of Kansas, Kansas Public Library Services, 2009 Statistics, www.kslib.info/statistics/index.html.

5. U.S. Census Bureau, State and County Quickfacts, http://quickfacts.census.gov/qfd/states/47/47113.html.

6. City-Data.com, http://www.city-data.com/county/Madison_County-TN.html.

7. City of Calabasas website, www.cityofcalabasas.com/stats.html.

8. California State Library, "California Library Statistics 2011."

9. Population figure from City-Data.com. Household income for States: 2009 and 2010, American Community Survey Briefs, September 2010, www.census.gov/prod/2010pubs/acsbr09-2.pdf.

10. Massachusetts Board of Library Commissioners, www.countingopinions.com/pireports/report.php?d7ecd2165468cb11a0dd94d04f4db207.

11. Population from City of Bedford website, www.ci.bedford.tx.us/ecodev/demographics.htm. Household income from www.city-data.com/city/Bedford-Texas.html, and American Community Survey Briefs, www.census.gov/prod/2010pubs/acsbr09-2.pdf.

12. Texas State Library, "Texas Public Library Statistics for 2009," www.tsl.state.tx.us/ld/pubs/pls/2009/plsstats.php.

4
KEY ISSUES FOR LIBRARIES FACING PRIVATIZATION

As the trend toward privatization of public assets is gaining traction in the conservative, cash-strapped climate of the 2010s, there is no doubt that this trend includes public libraries. Now that local governments across the country (and their library boards) are aware that privatizing their libraries is an option that may—at least at first glance—reduce costs, improve service, or both, a growing number of libraries will face the possibility of private management.

If you have not already had a trustee or council member raise the topic of privatizing libraries, you may soon. And when privatization is mentioned, it may be more than a casual conversation; more and more library directors find that their governing bodies are serious about exploring private management options.

The simplest piece of advice for this scenario is, simply, be prepared. ALA has made preparation easy by providing a series of steps and advice in their 2011 publication *Keeping Public Libraries Public: A Checklist for Communities Considering Privatization of Public Libraries*. The most relevant portions of that publication appear in this book's appendix, and this chapter expands on some of the advice. Use the information here to inform yourself and to consider carefully what needs to be understood and communicated in order to help your governing body make the best decision for your community.

WHAT PRIVATIZATION WILL MEAN FOR YOUR LIBRARY

If your public library were to change from public management to private, what would happen? For staff, library patrons, and the community as a whole, a privatized library means different things.

Under New Management

In a typical privatized library, the library director, along with the rest of the staff, is an employee of the management company and reports to an off-site manager at a headquarters or regional office. At the same time, she must report to the library's governing body—now the client of her employer—to ensure that the company is meeting their needs and expectations. Depending on the individual library, this reporting structure may work smoothly or may lead to communication breakdowns and staff feelings of disengagement from local government.

The library's processes naturally change as well. The management company handles "head office" functions, including payroll and human relations. The company may also take over library functions such as resource selection and purchasing or selecting and purchasing computer systems for both public access stations and staff; even reciprocal borrowing agreements may be altered. Longtime vendors may be replaced and traditional procedures changed.

Big Changes for Staff

One of the areas most affected by shifting a public library to private management is the staff. Upon privatization, all current library staff members have their government employment terminated and may be rehired by the new library contractor. (Of course, the contractor does not guarantee current employees a job, and employees are free to decide not to seek employment under the new arrangement.) This process includes interviewing for one's current position or other steps of a typical job application. Private contracting definitely includes a change in employment benefits. All government benefits, including vesting in government-managed pensions, disappear, to be replaced with the new employer's health insurance coverage, retirement package, and salary range.

Although data are unavailable on salaries and benefits offered by private management companies, it seems certain that library employees who work for these companies receive lower pay and lesser benefits. The fact that contractors must reduce or realign costs within a library's existing budget indicates that benefits or salaries—the largest expenses in running a library—must be reduced. An October 2010 article in *Library Journal* provides an example:

> In its proposal to run the Stockton-San Joaquin Public Library . . . LSSI said "professional level hires would typically start around $40,000, increasing to $55,000 or higher depending on education, experience, and level of responsibility." That is not comparable to current salaries, however. Under San Joaquin's current system, a Librarian I earns $45,338 to $58,204 a year, while a Librarian II earns $55,362 to $71,082 annually.[1]

Union library employees whose employer changes under privatization are no longer represented by public service unions such as Service Employees International Union. The employees would have to form a new bargaining unit in the "new" privately managed workplace.

If newly rehired staff members are unhappy with changes under their new employer, the company may prohibit them from speaking publicly about their feelings; a "gag order" may be included in terms of their employment.

WHAT PRIVATIZATION WILL MEAN FOR YOUR COMMUNITY

In many cases when a public library has been privatized, its typical patron remains unaware of the change. Library cards still work, materials are still there for the borrowing, the Wi-Fi connection is just as fast—but privatizing definitely results in some differences.

With new management comes a new budget (though total funding may remain the same), new goals or performance measures, and all the changes necessary to fulfill the new budget and goals. In cases where a government contracts with private management to trim costs, the community may see hours of operation reduced, staff cut, or even branches closed. In cases where a government contracts with private management for help reaching specific goals or improving service, the opposite may occur—the collection may grow rapidly, a new branch open, or broader programming be offered.

Loss of Community

The users of a newly privatized public library that was previously part of a larger system such as the county library could lose access to shared resources, such as specialty collections within the system. Or users may have access to the same materials but face a longer wait for these items.

The change can also reduce patrons' access to reciprocal borrowing within the former system. Depending on the contract and the state system, it is possible that members of the community may no longer be able to check materials out of neighboring libraries—or they may lose priority in requesting popular materials.

Loss of Transparency

As with any institution of local government, a public library automatically offers transparency. Members of its community (and others) can access information on budgets, meeting minutes, and decision making to see how the library spends their tax dollars and makes policy decisions.

But when a library is managed privately, that transparency does not transfer. The governing body's decisions remain transparent, but important factors that fall under the contractor's purview do not. These factors include details about library revenues, expenditures, and services. This loss of transparency means that future management review will be more difficult, because governments cannot determine cost efficiency and effectiveness if they do not have detailed information.

WHEN THE PROCESS BEGINS

Is your local government already considering privatization? Follow these steps to ensure that your leadership—staff and board—are involved in shaping the decision:

- Insist on an RFP process before a decision is made. Request input or review of what is included in the RFP, and provide recommendations on how to distribute the RFP.
- Provide as much detail on the library as possible to encourage a customized RFP. This should include all data you have on library usage and your patrons, the collection, staffing, budget, capital expenditures, and so forth. Keep in mind that the RFP for your library management will become the basis for the final contract

that specifies responsibilities, performance measures, and the like for the private firm.

Respond to the RFP

If you want your library to remain under public management, insist that your library staff be allowed to present a proposal in response to the RFP. This will effectively be your last chance to retain public control of the library, and that goal deserves a lot of time and attention.

Make sure you avoid a conflict of interest at this stage. You can suggest that several members of your board assist in writing and distributing the RFP but absent themselves from contributing to your staff proposal, or you can request that your governing body bring in a library specialist to help create and review the RFP.

The following steps supplement those listed in section VII of *Keeping Public Libraries Public:*

- Focus on the underlying issue. As a leader within your library, you must be aware of the reasons your governing body is seeking vendors. Whether it is concern over maintaining service levels on a shrinking budget, downward trends in circulation/visit numbers, or staff's resistance to change, pay special attention in your proposal to solving that problem. And be prepared to offer an option for radical change, if necessary—an outside vendor will not hesitate to do so.
- Make it a group effort. To create the best proposal, request input from your staff, colleagues, and board members. Let them review what you have at every stage. Ask friends from the corporate world to read the final draft and give you their input.
- Don't be afraid to be comprehensive. As long as you cover every point you want to make concisely, the more detail you are able to present, the better. Keep in mind that, if your proposal is solid and comprehensive, your governing body may use portions of it to create the final management contract—even if that contract goes to another bidder.

To truly compete, your proposal must match or exceed the quality of the others submitted. Specifically, it must be businesslike, comprehensive, and impartial.

QUESTIONS AND CUSTOMARY COURTESY

Note that when an RFP is out for bid from multiple vendors there is a customary courtesy in answering questions. If one bidder asks your governing body a question regarding response to the RFP, that body should share the answer with all bidders. Make sure your board or council is aware of this practice, and ensure that you are receiving any answers they share with other bidders.

Businesslike: Put aside any personal concerns or fears regarding a change in management at your library, and keep your tone and language purely businesslike throughout. Review similar proposals you find online or through library contacts, and mirror those you think are good. If you have a chance to present the proposal in person, dress, act, and respond to questions in a businesslike manner. If you include predictions of what will happen under privatization (such as cessation of reciprocal borrowing agreements), make sure they are actual and not prospective. Raising negative possibilities that are unlikely to occur can be easily identified as such, embarrassing you.

Comprehensive: The single most important success factor in a "winning" proposal is to make sure it addresses every element listed in the RFP. Make it clear to reviewers that you have done this by structuring your proposal so that its sections follow the order of those in the RFP exactly. You can even use the same headings (or terms and phrases) as the RFP.

Impartial: Is your board or governing body accustomed to hearing or reading reports from the library director? If so, make sure this proposal does not seem like "business as usual." Subtle changes include using different paper, fonts, and formats; change the writing style if appropriate. When drafting the proposal, put yourself in the frame of mind of a consultant from a different community. Label yourself or your group consistently throughout the document—"Everytown Public Library Management (EPLM)"—and do not refer to decisions or actions made in the past unless they are relevant to your point.

Make the Contract Count

After a decision is made and a contractor selected, a contract is drawn up. This contract is based on both the RFP and the proposal of the selected vendor—but that does not mean that additional items cannot be negotiated before the agreement is finalized. As mentioned in chapter 3, most of the contracts we examined were actually provided by the vendor. Regardless of who drafts the initial document, the library board should insist that the final contract be as specific as possible about expected outcomes and performance measures, as opposed to a list of work to be performed.

"A Checklist for Contract Consideration," in part IV of *Keeping Public Libraries Public*, lists essential provisions to include in any library management contract, including several performance measures. Share this list with your governing body, your board, and any other decision makers involved in finalizing the contract.

Encourage the decision makers to replace any vague or "cookie-cutter" language on points of responsibility and performance with specifics. For example, the contract should specify that the library must meet or exceed the previous year's performance on state and national performance measures.

Review the contract for any policy changes that would lead to superficially good but misleading performance measures, such as shortening the loan period from three weeks to two, which typically increases circulation and gate numbers as patrons return to renew materials.

Carefully review any reductions in budget to ascertain their true impact on services. If you see a discrepancy, ask for details that are more specific on how objectives will be met under the budget line item.

IN CONCLUSION

One final overarching piece of advice for those interested in monitoring the trend of privatization of public libraries: stay informed. Keep an eye out for privatization news in industry media, or set up a Google alert to receive any new postings on "public libraries" and "private management." Over time, note where the trend is moving. Are libraries that have privatized doing well? Are they renewing their contracts? Have new players entered the game? Has the trend begun to plateau or decline? Collect statistics and examples, and soon you will have information to answer any questions from your governing body, board, patrons, or colleagues.

NOTE

1. Michael Kelley, "LSSI Wins New Contract in California," *Library Journal,* October 19, 2010, www.libraryjournal.com/lj/home/887353-264/lssi_wins_new_contract_in.html.csp.

The following is taken verbatim from *Keeping Public Libraries Public: A Checklist for Communities Considering Privatization of Public Libraries*, published in 2011 by the Office for Library Advocacy, American Library Association.

A Checklist for Considering Privatization

Deciding to privatize public library management and operations is a critical decision that can have unforeseen consequences or an impact beyond what is expected, and be divisive within a community. It is important that a governing body (library board, city council, or county commission) consider multiple aspects of this decision. This checklist presents issues that should be discussed by a governing body prior to making this crucial decision. Governing boards should consider each question in light of its relevance to their local communities.

Funding

- How much money will the contract save? Has the library staff been asked if they can produce an equal amount of savings?
- How much profit margin will the company expect?
- Could profit paid to the company, combined with new library efficiencies, preserve public control of the library?
- How will the governing body monitor and verify that the anticipated cost savings occurred without damage to library services?
- Does the proposed contract include costs to fully manage the library—for example, the costs of rent, building and ground maintenance, and utilities?
- What are the costs of exiting any existing vendor or other cooperative contracts if the private company cancels them?
- What are the costs of canceling the contract if the privatization service is not satisfactory? Can the city retain staff hired by the private company?

Library Services

- Will the same range of services be offered? Will services (including hours and locations) be decreased in number of offerings or frequency?

- Some services incur greater expenses for resources while others are very staff intensive. If forced to reduce, eliminate, or initiate services, will the private company be able to make informed decisions, mindful of the needs of the community?

- Will community input be solicited?

- What specific improvements in public service will result from the contract? How will the company pay for these improvements?

- Who, specifically, will evaluate that the library is providing the same or better library service? What specific criteria will be used in this determination?

- Will reciprocal borrowing (the ability to borrow from other libraries in the region) be continued, or will local library users be denied quick access to materials in other libraries? If these privileges are removed, will the library still participate in interlibrary loan agreements?

- Will the company engage in strategic planning?

- Will current library staff be retained? Experienced and dedicated library staff is the heart of library services to a community. Staff costs are the largest percentage of any organization's budget. Therefore, how a private company will handle staff costs must be understood before a contract is signed. What will the staffing patterns of the library be when it becomes privatized? How many full- and part-time staff will be employed?

- Will the hours and benefits of current staff be reduced? If so, by how much?

- Will existing employment contracts be honored?

Community Control

- Will there continue to be a library board, and will it continue to have the same level of authority and responsibility authorized in state law? Who will make library policies regarding such areas as the ability of children to use the Internet, or the setting of fees and fines?

- Will policy remain under local control? What is the role of the board of trustees? Will existing trustees continue to have whatever authority is given them in state law?

- To whom is the director of a privatized library accountable?

- Who will develop the library's collection to meet the needs of the local community?

- Will corporate staff at the company's headquarters make decisions about what goes in the library's collection? What input will the public and library staff have?

- What input will the community have when the contract is up for renewal? How will community satisfaction be determined? How will the community be informed of library plans, budgets, and performance? Will Friends, foundations, and other entities be able to continue to operate and provide financial support under their present structures?

- How will the community know where their library tax money is spent and what amount goes to company profit?

Political Questions

- Have library governing or advisory boards been involved in planning and decision making? Does the library governing or advisory board support the privatization decision?

- Has the local community been involved in the privatization decision-making process? Has the community been asked what library services they prefer? Does the community support privatization of the library?

- How will the library reestablish public management of the library if the private company is not satisfactory?

Organization and Staff

- Does the company propose a change to the organizational structure of the library? Will library staff be retained?

- If current employees are not rehired by the company, what is the city's financial or human resource obligation to them? Who pays unemployment, retirement, or other termination costs? How will the city or county pay for legal defense arising from employment issues?

- Will volunteers replace existing trained staff?

- How will the company train volunteers and pay for any associated workmen's compensation insurance?

- Will company hiring practices include recruiting a diverse population to match the makeup of the community?

- If the contract with the private company ends, can the governing body retain library staff without paying a finder's fee to the company?

Legal

- How will compliance to all library-specific federal, state, and local laws and regulations be addressed?

- How will current collective bargaining contracts, employee benefits, and related issues be handled?

- Has a search of legal records been done to determine if there are any liens or judgments against the company?

- Has the potential impact on directors' and officers' insurance been investigated?

A Checklist for Contract Consideration

What should be considered when soliciting a proposal and developing a contract for a public library? A private company may indicate that it cannot answer these questions until it has begun to manage the library. However, a discussion with the private company should include the governing authority's intentions. The same questions should be asked of the local library as a competitor for the contract, which would keep the library fully under public control.

Contract Provisions

- Frequency and content of regular reports to the governing body
- Oversight of the contract by governing body staff or officials
- Performance measures to ensure quality performance such as:

  Circulation and circulation per capita (print, electronic, CD/DVD, etc.)

  Community presentations

  Number of individuals served through outreach services

  Registration as percentage of population

  Reference transactions and reference transactions per capita (on-site, phone, and virtual reference)

  In-library use, visits (walk-in traffic, computer usage)

  Web visits, database usage

  Interlibrary loan statistics

  Program attendance

  Number of programs by month and year

  Growth or decline of existing services

  Establishment of new services to meet community needs

  Hours open, total and by day

  Status in relation to any state standards

  The ratio between full-time and part-time staff

  The ratio between librarians with an MLS degree and staff without MLS degrees

  Number of volunteers and volunteer hours

  Holds-to-copy ratio

  Return on Investment

  Services offered to different demographics (i.e., teen services, emergent literacy, ESOL)

- Criteria governing cancellation of the contract for performance issues
- Areas of library service where profit may be realized at the expense of quality. Degree to which any state standards must be met, i.e., no less than before privatization or above average for peer libraries

- Ability to retain library staff without paying a finder's fee to the private company if the contract is cancelled

- Company adherence to all applicable state library law, including privacy of library records and use

- Any protections for current library staff jobs, salaries, or benefits

- Degree of transparency that the private company will provide about its financial operation of the library, particularly its profit margin

Action Steps for Libraries and Their Supporters

If Privatization Is Being Considered

Privatization of public libraries has become an option that is being considered by some cities and counties (governing bodies). The American Library Association has taken a position against such privatization, particularly on a long-term basis. Library staff and their supporters—boards of trustees, Friends groups, library foundations—play a major role in keeping public libraries public. Here are four steps one can take if privatization is being considered.

- Be an advocate.
- Be informed.
- Be prepared.
- Be competitive.

Be an Advocate

The best defense against privatization of public libraries is for the library staff and supporters to maintain a good relationship with the library's governing body and operate the most efficient library possible while providing the best possible service to meet the community's needs. Libraries maintain good relations by:

- Demonstrating the value of the library in addressing community needs
- Delivering quality customer service to meet community needs
- Cultivating vocal community support for the library
- Being in regular, positive contact with governing officials
- Sharing good news about library successes
- Involving governing officials in library activities
- Regularly improving library operation and letting the governing officials know about these improvements

Learning advocacy skills is the first step in becoming an effective advocate. The American Library Association, the Public Library Association, state associations, and state libraries offer training and other resources. If governing officials are pleased with the library and aware of strong public support, the issue of privatizing the public library is not as likely to arise.

Be Informed

The legal authority of a library board of trustees may vary depending on specific state statutes. However, as guardians of a public trust, all trustees have an obligation to understand their duties and obligations to the communities they serve. Citizens for Libraries: The Association of Library Trustees, Advocates, Friends and Foundations has developed a list of 10 trustee competencies that are essential to performing the job of a trustee. The question of privatization is less likely to occur if the library trustees demonstrate their knowledge and expertise of these competencies. The competencies are general knowledge; board operation; advocacy; decision making; strategic planning; finance; fundraising; policy making; lobbying; and professional development. (For more information, visit http://www.ala.org/ala/mgrps/divs/altaff/trustees/tipsheets/tipsheet9.pdf.) Ongoing board development and education are essential to maintaining a knowledgeable board.

Be Prepared

All library advocates must be prepared for the question of whether or not privatizing the local public library could be in the best interest of the community. In these days of limited financial resources, every public service must justify its value to the public it serves. Transparency and accountability are paramount. Library trustees and administrators must continually document and validate library services and expenditures. This documentation may also prove essential in providing an accurate comparison between the cost of current library service and privatized service.

When the idea of privatizing public libraries arises, library advocates should be prepared to counter the idea in a timely manner and thoroughly analyze why privatization is being considered. Do governing officials lack key information about the library? Do governing officials know the extent of library services?

Some public officials are intrigued with the idea of privatization but do not really understand all that privatization entails or what its implications can be. Library staff should share ALA's Checklist for Considering Privatization. This checklist will give a better understanding of what should be considered in privatization decisions.

The better prepared a library is to show its value to the community, the better the chance of deflecting privatization before governing officials seriously consider it. Advocates should collect and update the information listed below. If one waits until privatization is at hand, there might not be enough time to gather the necessary documentation to show the value of the library. An additional benefit of gathering this information is that it can support current advocacy efforts with governing officials, the public, the press, and other stakeholders. Here are the kinds of information to have readily available:

- A long-range or strategic plan of service that shows that the library continually considers the best way to provide library service for the community

- Recent audits showing improvements in fiscal management that have saved the library money and how the saved money was spent to improve library service
- Staffing levels and responsibilities of professional and support staff
- Data on library use over time for common library uses such as resource circulation, reference, and programming
- A complete list of all library services, including use over time and any information on favorable reception by the public
- Any data profile that is required by the state
- Comparisons of the local library to its peers showing its success in providing service with limited resources, if possible
- Testimonial from library users about their satisfaction with the local library and the quality of service they receive
- Accomplishments of the library over the last two or three years
- Cooperative ventures and partnerships in place to better serve library users
- Involvement of Friends, foundations, and other support groups.

If governing officials are philosophically in favor of working with private companies or cooperative ventures to save money, library staff and trustees might show that they are already seriously involved in outsourcing, but that library governance and policymaking should remain in the public sector. Libraries commonly outsource services in the following areas:

Collection development: Materials may be ordered already processed from a private vendor so that library staff does not have to do this; similarly, databases may be provided by private companies, saving the library money in print magazine subscriptions. However, library staff still have the critical responsibility of collection development.

Programming: The library contracts with private performers and speakers to provide programming for adults and youth.

Building maintenance: Janitorial and building maintenance might be outsourced.

Ancillary services: Technology support, accounting, payroll, benefits management might be outsourced.

Be Competitive

If the library's governing body has released a Request for Proposals (RFP) for library services, a response on behalf of the library should also be submitted. If the library responds to the RFP:

- Read the RFP thoroughly. Be ready to respond to every section in the RFP as comprehensively as possible. Try to determine the reason for the interest in privatizing the library. Is it to save money? If so, demonstrate that the current library administration and trustees can be responsive to the continuing need for efficiency in library operation. Is it lack of awareness of the performance of the library in the community? If so, document this performance in the RFP response.
- Review the documents collected in "Be Prepared" to see if they contain information necessary to respond to the RFP. Add whatever additional information is missing.
- Review the RFP and responses to ensure that the proposal answers all the questions in the RFP.
- Create a calendar and a work plan to respond to the RFP. Pay attention to deadlines. Also plan to implement any changes in library services and operations that are mentioned in the RFP.
- Solicit letters of support from influential community members, representatives of important community groups, Friends groups, the library trustees, and demographic groups. Follow the RFP process closely. If a private company is given an opportunity to submit additional information or a revised budget, ask for the same privilege for the library. If possible, obtain legal advice on the required RFP process and procedures and verify that the governing body is following these correctly.

If Privatization Is Being Pursued

If the governing authority has decided to privatize the local public library, the new goal is to ensure quality library service for the community. Here are two steps one can take if privatization is being pursued.

1. Insist on accountability in the contract.

First, share the checklist on what should go into a contract with governing officials, executive staff, and appropriate legal counsel. Assuming the contract is a public document, library supporters can raise issues about the contract content to ensure the highest possible library service.

Second, the contract should specify performance-measurement indicators prior to privatization and require that those measurements are compared in regular increments throughout the contract period.

2. Monitor all new library policies and administrative activities.

Monitor any privatization contracts to make sure service to the public does not suffer. The contract should specify areas that should be monitored on a regular basis, including:

- Adherence to and adoption of library policy
- Payment of bills
- Adherence to all library contracts
- Adherences to state library law and standards
- Adherence to or development of a strategic plan
- Appropriate use of grants
- Cost-cutting measures do not negatively impact service
- Community comments or suggestions and the company's responses to them are forwarded to the governing board

If the state library or state library law have standards for public libraries, monitor the company's performance to ensure that the library meets or exceeds these standards, and that library performance in relation to the standards does not deteriorate after privatization.

Make sure that each board member has a copy of any recently developed long-range or strategic plan and watches to see that all elements of the plan are being addressed and that positive progress is being made, or that the for-profit company is providing information relative to any deviations. Be sure that the governing board is involved in any revisions to the plan.

In addition:

- Be sure that staff receives continuing education or on-the-job training to ensure quality public service.

- The company should receive an annual performance review based on the contract.

- If deficiencies are found, an action plan for remediation within a specific time frame should be developed.

- Watch for cost-cutting measures such as employing mostly part-time employees and/or using volunteers for work that should be done by paid staff. When such measures are noted, be cognizant of how they affect library services and activities. Require that the for-profit company provide monthly copies of all community input received and an explanation of actions taken by the company in relation to each.

- Develop other methods for monitoring community response to the new library set-up and related actions taken by the company.

- Review all points above and determine exactly what action will be taken by the board or by city or county government in the event that the for-profit fails to meet requirements and expectations. How long will the company be given to correct any problem? Will there be any penalty fee charged to the company if there is a problem but it is corrected? How will the board establish an appropriate level of correction in each case?

BIBLIOGRAPHY

American Library Association. *Keeping Public Libraries Public: A Checklist for Communities Considering Privatization of Public Libraries.* Chicago: American Library Association, 2011. www.ala.org/ala/professionalresources/outsourcing/ALAKeepingPublicLibrariesPublicFINAL0611.pdf.

_____. "Outsourcing and Privatization in American Libraries." Report by ALA Outsourcing Task Force, January 6, 1999. www.ala.org/ala/aboutala/offices/oif/iftoolkits/outsourcing/outsourcingamericanlibs.cfm.

Baxandall, Phineas. "Is Privatizing Roads Really a Solution to Our Transportation Budget Woes?" *The Infrastructurist.* www.infrastructurist.com/2009/04/08/is-privatizing-roads-really-a-solution-to-our-transportation-budget-woes.

California Library Association. "A Letter to CLA Membership." California Library Association, 2011.

Florida House of Representatives Committee on Tourism. "Report on Privatization of Public Libraries: Pros and Cons. www.leg.state.fl.us/publications/2001/house/reports/tourism/lib_pdfs/exe_sum.pdf.

Florida Library Association. "Florida Public Libraries and Privatization: A Guide for Florida Library Boards and Friends." Florida State Library, Tallahassee, 2000.

Gilroy, Leonard. "Local Government Privatization 101." Reason Foundation. http://reason.org/news/printer/local-government-privatization-101.

Hartmann, Meg Klinkow. "Show Me the Money: Privatization and the Public Library." *ILA Reporter,* February 2011.

Hill, Heather. "Outsourcing the Public Library: A Critical Discourse Analysis." Ph.D. diss., Information Science and Learning Technologies, University of Missouri, 2009. https://mospace.umsystem.edu/xmlui/bitstream/handle/10355/6126/research.pdf?sequence=3.

International City-County Management Association. *Profile in Local Government Service Delivery Choices.* Washington, DC: ICMA, 2007.

In the Public Interest. "A Guide to Evaluating Public Asset Privatization." www.inthepublicinterest.org/article/guide-evaluating-public-asset-privatization. In the Public Interest, 2011.

Killoran, Maureen. "Privatization of Public Libraries: A List of Information Resources." Massachusetts Board of Library Commissioners, Boston, 2008.

Martin, R. S. *The Impact of Outsourcing and Privatization on Library Services and Management.* Chicago: American Library Association, 2000.

Maynard, Melissa. "Outsourcing the Local Library Can Lead to a Loud Backlash." *Stateline,* August 1, 2011. www.stateline.org/live/printable/story?contentId=591002.

New Jersey Library Association Executive Board. "Statement on Outsourcing Public Library Services." NJLA, 2001.

Nichols, Russell. "The Pros and Cons of Privatizing Government Functions." Governing.com, December 2010. www.governing.com/topics/mgmt/pros-cons-privatizing-government-functions.html.

Oder, Norman. "When LSSI Comes to Town." *Library Journal* 129, no. 16 (2004): 36–42.

Pioneer Institute for Public Policy Research. "Competition & Government Services: Can Massachusetts Still Afford the Pacheco Law?" Boston, 2002.

Poole, Robert W., Jr. "Ronald Reagan and the Privatization Revolution." *Heartlander,* August 1, 2004. www.heartland.org/policybot/results/15469/Ronald_Reagan_and_the_Privatization_Revolution.html.

State Environmental Resource Center. Water Privatization Fact Pack, updated September 25, 2004. www.serconline.org/waterPrivatization/fact.html.

Sylvain, Matt. "Library Professional Speaks Out on Possible Library Privatization." *Southcoast Today/ Chronicle,* January 28, 2009.

Wallin, Bruce. *Privatization of State Services in Massachusetts: Politics, Policy, and an Experiment That Wasn't.* Department of Political Science, Northeastern University, for the Economic Policy Institute, Washington, DC, 1995.

Ward, R. C. "The Outsourcing of Public Library Management: An Analysis of the Application of New Public Management Theories from the Principal-Agent Perspective." *Administration and Society* 38 (2007): 627–648.

INDEX

You may also be interested in

GRASSROOTS LIBRARY ADVOCACY

Lauren Comito, Aliqae Geraci, and Christian Zabriskie

This ALA Editions Special Report cuts through the rhetoric and gets straight to modeling a plan of action, for libraries big and small, by detailing the lessons learned during the authors' successful campaign to save New York City libraries; instructing readers how to clarify their message, manage volunteers, and plan events; and offering public relations strategies, including advice for dealing with political leaders and the media.

ISBN: 978-0-8389-1134-1
80 pages / 8.5" x 11"

A LIBRARIAN'S GUIDE TO AN UNCERTAIN JOB MARKET
Jeannette Woodward
ISBN: 978-0-8389-1105-1

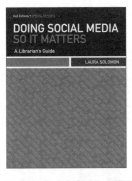

DOING SOCIAL MEDIA SO IT MATTERS: A LIBRARIAN'S GUIDE
Laura Solomon
ISBN: 978-0-8389-1067-2

OPEN ACCESS: WHAT YOU NEED TO KNOW NOW
Walt Crawford
ISBN: 978-0-8389-1106-8

GOING MOBILE: DEVELOPING APPS FOR YOUR LIBRARY USING BASIC HTML PROGRAMMING
Scott La Counte
ISBN: 978-0-8389-1129-7

GRANT MONEY THROUGH COLLABORATIVE PARTNERSHIPS
Nancy Kalikow Maxwell
ISBN: 978-0-8389-1159-4

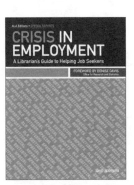

CRISIS IN EMPLOYMENT: A LIBRARIAN'S GUIDE TO HELPING JOB SEEKERS
Jane Jerrard with a foreword by Denise Davis, Office for Research and Statistics (ORS)
ISBN: 978-0-8389-1013-9